ALL FOUR CHAPTERS
(My First Forty Years)

STACI MARINEZ

This is a work of non-fiction. All events of this book are told to the best of my memory in how I saw the truth.

ALL FOUR CHAPTERS
(My First Forty Years)

All rights reserved.

Published by PaigeOne
Copyright© 2015 by Staci Marinez
Cover by Staci Marinez

ISBN: 9781517317379
ISBN: 1571317371

First Printing: September 2015
Printed in the United States of America

Dedicated To: Everyone who has

fallen, but gotten back up.

ACKNOWLEDGEMENTS

My Heavenly Father, for giving me the strength and courage to get back up when I fell down. Through God all things are possible, His blessings are ever present in my life and His favor is ours to claim.

Tahlia (Boogie): Baby girl, you are God's most precious gift to me. Being your mother has given me more joy than I could have ever imagined. My love for you is endless and immeasurable. You are and have always been an exemplary daughter, even when my life was cloudy and out of control. You steadfast with a caring hand and beautiful words of encouragement. My life would be simply ordinary if not for you. Please know that of all the things I've experienced in this world, you are and will always be my greatest accomplishment and the greatest miracle, here on earth.

iv

My Mother and Father, for giving me life. You have played a pivotal role in who I've become. I want you to know that I am forever her daughter and will love you both unconditionally for as long as I draw breath.

Sister Sledge: You are my angel here on earth. Your care and love has never wavered and though you have always chose to take the back seat, your heart is bigger than any I have encountered.

Morgan: Wow, who knew that you would need to be big sister rather than little sister at times. I am so very proud of you and the woman you have become. My appreciation for the love and support you have provided me over the years cannot be put into words, but know that you are a true life saver.

Liza: Our 20 years of friendship has seen its fair share of happiness and mishap. We've been each other's rock as well as partners in crime. We have "take it to the graves" and memories that are ours and ours alone. Although God tested your faith by taking sweet Geremy home, He makes no mistakes. We now have another personal angel to watch over and protect us.

Treva: Thanks for the encouragement to keep writing. Girl, you know that you were heaven sent to me. The talks, your genuine heart and for all your prayers, Thank you!

My other 2 daughters: Amber and Maddie, it's been a pleasure to watch you two grow into beautiful young ladies, may your futures be ever so bright. I love you girls.

TABLE OF CONTENTS

INTRODUCTION

I recently reached a point in my life and realized that it's time to use the lessons learned to propel myself into a more positive future. This ordeal has had a major impact on my here and now. How enlightening it has been to take time out to reflect on the meaning of one's life. The purpose for this book was to do some overdue internal house cleaning, but after a few days of prayer and a talk with my daughter, the decision was made to publish. In doing this I can only hope that someone out there will learn that no matter what life throws at you, it is possible to get back up. Whether you call on God, a friend, reach out to family or seek professional help a new day can be had.

A very profound fact was brought to the forefront of my mind while writing this story. Though capable of making my own life choices, I allowed the circumstances of the past to perpetuate, rather than forge new pathways. The effect that dysfunction has on all involved in the family sect can cause everlasting damage that some people never overcome, but if we are lucky the cycle can be broken. It may take years to make this discovery but as long as it is made the chance for peace and happiness are possible, which is in my opinion one of life's greatest rewards. To share this story with family, friends and others has shown me just how strong the human spirit can be.

CHAPTER 1
Dysfunction Through the Eyes of a Child

I have always been fascinated by the moment we first become aware of our existence. What is it that brings about the recall of our first childhood memories? I remember scenes from several different times in three different states. Dad was from Ohio, Mom from Kansas, and Missouri – where my mom's brother lived – was one of our runaway places. All from the ripe old age of five. Some of these memories are good, but the bad ones always seem to overshadow them. What amazes me is that I recall more happening in that year than in all the years that followed. Although I can't remember the exact order in which the events occurred, the experiences themselves are extremely vivid even today.

Running through the house, Mom instructed all of us kids: "Put your shoes on, and go to the car."

My cousin and I were playing that morning because he had slept over for the night. That was one of the nice things about being back in the Midwest: there were lots of family and friends we could play with. Not all of them were my cousins. We just called each other that because our moms and dads had been friends for such a long time. Mom finally got us in the car and we were off. Off to where, I had no idea, but man, she was driving fast! It was like being on a roller coaster ride at an amusement park. I thought she was a really good driver because of the way she took that turn into the trailer park.

Once the dust cleared and the car came to a stop, Mom jumped out. Everything was moving so fast. One minute she was behind the car getting something out of the trunk, then the next thing I knew she was running toward the trailer with this long metal rod in her hand – a tire iron. What came next was like

11

something out of a TV movie. Mom ran around that little white trailer and broke out all the windows she could reach. I could hear her screaming, "Come out! Get out here, you dirty %#$@!&% – you and your little !@#$%!" She was angry, and I still didn't understand what she was doing or why, but all my confusion cleared up when Dad parted that front door, butt-naked, telling Mom, "You need to calm down and go home."

Before we knew it, the cops were there and everyone was screaming and cussing at one another. It was a big ol' mess.

Moving on to the next episode...

Mom and Auntie sat in the front seats, and all of us silly, crazy kids piled in the back. If I'm not mistaken, I think we're in the same car that we used in the trailer park riot. We are out for a simple drive around town to get ice cream or something – not sure exactly, but I can feel the steady bumps and jolts from the cobblestone road beneath the car.

It was a little country town in the south-west tip of Kansas, where everyone knew everyone. Main Street was only four blocks long, but it boasted a one-screen walk-up movie theater, a Woolworth's, a few other shops and a boutique called Vogue. I remember admiring the fancy dresses in the window and thinking that one day I would grow up and do my shopping in that store instead of down the street at Sears or Penny's, where Mom purchased most of our clothes. Not that I was complaining by any means. On the contrary. Because Mom didn't just treat us with a store visit downtown – she was a dedicated subscriber to the department stores' catalogs. So the days when the mailman would plop a big brown box on our front porch were like Christmas for my sister and me.

We had left Granny's house only a short time earlier. We turned down the street where the Knights of Columbus was and, what do you know, there was dear ole Dad and some white girl, out for a bike ride. They were riding the-his-and-hers bikes that belonged to my parents. Well, my dad was on his and, unfortunately, for the girl, she was on my mom's. Before a word could be spoken, the little brown car came to an abrupt halt once again. In one fell swoop, Mom was out of the car and across the street. That poor girl didn't have a chance. With absolute ease, Mom snatched her off the bike and dragged her several feet by her hair. I don't remember what those of us in the car did or said, but I'm sure dropped jaws and shocked faces were plastered out of each window to see the spectacle transpiring before our eyes. Now, what makes this even worse is the fact that my dad took off and left that poor thing to fend for herself.

As I look back, bits and pieces come to me, but I don't think I will ever be able to remember all of it. I am well aware that there are things I know, but which my mind has chosen to block out permanently.

Still, there are plenty of memories that will stay with me forever. Case in point, the moving back and forth: Midwest is home, then up North, next the Midwest again, and we must not forget the sunny West Coast. I was always asked, "Is your father in the military?" When I would say "No," the next question would be, "Then why all the moving around?" With a small hint of shame, void of hesitation, my answer remained the same: "Dysfunction."

My parents had met when my dad was stationed in Fort Riley after returning from Vietnam. Story has it the relationship was doomed from the start. Why, you may ask. Well, as it's been told, my father and one of my mom's best friends "hooked-up" the night before the wedding. I want to say that she knew before walking down the aisle, but that just doesn't make any sense, does it? This was marriage number two for her. Not a good way to start off a new life, at all.

Even at this very young age, I knew something was wrong, broken if you will. It was trying, stressful, annoying and downright ridiculous to me. I'll expand on this later, but first I must explain that infidelity was the lesser of two evils that we witnessed.

We're back up north now in Dad's home state of Ohio. The town's main focal points are the industrial park where the big blue Whirlpool building sat and the state prison, which is said to have housed the notorious Don King at some point.

It started out as any other night at the dinner table. Exactly what started it, and why it started, Lord only knows. A sound, a look, dust on the floor too long. You never knew what was going to set him off.

They kept screaming at each other. This time, he actually pushed back from the dinner table and rises up out of his chair. With temples pulsing and finger pointed, Dad was in full explosive mode. Trust me, this was nothing new. The fights and disagreements were a constant staple in our home, and kept us walking on eggshells, doing our best not to upset or unnerve Daddy. At times, it consisted of hair pulling, choking, arm twisting, and head banging or just flat-out in-your-face. But he was no dummy, and was always careful not to leave face marks or bruises, so that if and when the law showed up he could plead, "What? Look at her. Besides tears, is there any evidence of abuse?" Terrified of his retaliation, Mom would remain quiet, and so the cops would eventually leave without action.

So, what made this different from previous nights? My sister and I were crying because it was just so loud and there was nothing we could do. Mom was frozen in her chair for fear of what would come next. With a swift forward thrust of his hand, Dad made contact and, as if in slow motion, Mom toppled backward out of her chair and landed on the floor; first her shoulders, then the thud of her head hitting the ground. We saw the tears begin to flow from her eyes. Family dinner was over. It was time to clean up and go to bed. To myself I would always say, "He's so mean. Why does he have to be so mean?"

The vicious cycle consisted of her leaving, him apologizing, then us returning. This happened over and over again. Once I recall us trying to get away on a bus heading out of town. I can't remember how far we got. I just know that he tracked down the bus, and for some strange reason the driver allowed him on board, where he proceeded to convince, threaten or whatever, Mom to come back home.

Now, this is what I mean by "absolutely ridiculous". Being under the age of ten and constantly witnessing this nonsense, I approached my mother and asked her, "Why on earth would you stay with this man?" Yes, this was my dad I was talking about, but ask me if I cared. It was stupid and the pure definition of insanity. But hey, what did I know? I was only a child, right?

Here I am, up north, and the weather is perfect. I am not sure of the season, but I know it feels really good to be sitting outside on the sidewalk, next to the house, with my music. With the help of an electric cord that I found in my dad's stuff, my little record player is all plugged in and ready to go.

There was nothing more important to me than my music, and it is still just as true today. I was so excited. No more carrying all those 45s around in a paper bag. Mom had bought me my very own portable record holder. Man, I had to be the luckiest little girl in the world! It had a baby blue lid and a white bottom with a cylinder ring over which the records would slide down. Of course, my holder also had a twist lock on top so that they wouldn't fall out while I carried it. I sat out there for hours listening and dancing around to my music. Not quite sure which songs were playing, just know that my baby blue and white case carried more than thirty 45s, and it was full.

It was my escape, you know. It was a way for me to turn off all the ugly noise and replace it with beautiful sounds and rhythms. It was my dream world. It was the place where I could disappear too, anytime and anywhere, if only for a little while.

Amidst the drama of my family life, I did relish the ability to be a kid. It wasn't always bad. We had family trips to amusement parks such as Cedar Point where the Whirlpool picnic was held every year, occasional family functions, and just the sheer joy of playing outside until the street lights came on. Those of you who grew up in my day know what would happen if you didn't make it home in time… you got your butt toasted. Ha ha! Classic things such as riding bikes, snowball fights and lying on skateboards in the middle of the street, which my cousin and I got a spanking for, were very happy times for me.

I fondly recall two bright, shiny ten-speed bikes, one sunshine yellow (for me) and the other brilliant blue (for my sister). They were perched on the front porch waiting for my sister and me upon our return from New York one summer after visiting our grandparents. I immediately carried my bike to the sidewalk, Mom and Dad smiling, trailing behind me. I hopped on and, with my parents' "Be careful" still in my ears, raced down the street directly into a tree. In those moments of youthful bliss, the dysfunction would be temporarily placed on the shelf, up out of my reach and out of sight.

1980, and it's time for a change in scenery. After being hit in the head and left to die in the snow for hustling some dude at the pool hall, Dad is laid up and broken. Honestly, I couldn't make this stuff up – my imagination is not that good! Now a family of five – Mom, Dad, my older sister who's now thirteen, I'm ten, and we have a new baby sister who is a month old – we pack- up, put the north in our rear-view mirror heading for the West Coast. Who knows? A new start could be just what we all need.

Yeah, right! Instead of getting better, the progression of decay and discontent was running ramped. The arguments and fighting continued, even in sunny California. The cross-country trip only changed the venue, not the cast members. Just when we thought it couldn't get any worse, it did. My father crossed a line that no father should ever cross.

One of the reasons my mother had stayed in such a vile marriage was because of her first-born, my sissy as I called her. She was three when they had gotten together, and not having her biological father in her life, she was raised by my mom and my dad. She carried his last name, for Christ's sake. She adored him. He was Daddy to her, and when things were bad she would beg my mother, "Please don't leave my daddy". The very man who would one day betray her trust and loyalty by kissing and groping her in the kitchen of our home, before driving her to a school field trip.

When he was confronted about the act, a fight ensued. I don't have all the details of what happened that night because we had been shuttled off to a movie, but what I can tell you is that when we got home, we were swiftly directed to remain in the car with my cousin's grandmother. All of the sudden, we saw my mom run out of the house and down the street, diving head first over the bushes at the end of the block. Following close behind was my dad. He could run like a gazelle at the time, but by the grace of God, he had not exited the house in time to see Mom's quick hedge maneuver. As he rounded the corner, still in chase mode, out came my aunt with a cooking fork! My auntie was fierce and didn't take any crap. He didn't dare confront her – she would have quickly turned him into a human kebab. This night gave a whole new meaning to the old saying "putting your business in the street".

At some point, all three of them ended up back in the house. Little did my dad know they were about to have company. Still with her wits about her before the fight escalated, Mom had taken Dad's gun and thrown it under the bed so that he would not have access to it. I firmly believe that one act saved both their lives that night. Her life because he was in such a rage that there was no telling what would have happened if he'd had a weapon. His life because if he'd had one, the boys in blue – who had already positioned themselves inside and around the house – would have blown him away. This may be the reason I like comedies more than any other type of movie. Horror and drama were available for free right in the comfort of my own home.

As offbeat as this may sound, something good actually came out of the madness of that night. After fourteen years of fear and excuses, my mother finally, *finally* left my father. We had to move into a women's shelter, but I didn't care. Anything was better than the way we'd been living. I'm not sure how long we stayed in the shelter. Its location was a well-kept secret to prevent anyone's mate or husband from finding out where they were. Strangely enough, I felt safe. Being among people I didn't know, whom I'd never seen before, gave me a sense of security. Somehow, it doesn't seem quite right, but that's how it was. Unfortunately, there was a limit to the time we could remain in the shelter, so our moment of peace was short-lived.

This was to be a whole new start for my sisters and me. Mom and Dad were over, or so we thought. The apartment complex that we lived in when we first got to California was once again home… for all of us. Mom and us girls lived on the left side, right next door to the apartment managers, and Dad – well, he was living in an end unit on the right, just across the parking lot. Let's just say that it was a little too close for comfort, in my opinion.

At this point, our ages were fourteen, eleven and one. As for me, being the middle child would put me in a very compromising position for many years to come.

Divorce was imminent, but things had actually calmed down between our parents, and it seemed amicable enough – until that night.

My sister was in the kitchen washing dishes; I was running around playing with my mom's roommate's kids, while the baby was having a snack in her high chair. We were all at my dad's and had the whole house to ourselves, but not for as long as we thought. Arriving back earlier than planned, Mom, her roommate and Dad walked through the door, and instantly you could have cut the tension with a knife. Not long after that, we heard raised voices coming from the back bedroom of my dad's apartment. You guessed it, they brought a fight that had started elsewhere back home.

One thing you should know is that my dad had a bad habit of bringing us kids into the argument with questions such as, "Did you see?" or "Remember when?" For some strange reason, he felt it would help his case, though it never did.

Out of the bedroom they came, screaming and yelling about who knows what, or why. Within minutes, the argument turned into a full-fledged disaster. All sister wanted to do was finish washing the dishes, but no, he kept at her. "Leave me alone," she said, more than once. Do you think he would listen? Nope. Not my dad.

From somewhere deep inside, my sister was able to find the strength and courage that Mom never had and POP! Right smack dab in the nose. The look on his face was priceless, dumbfounded and confused. Blood was running down his face. He disappeared into his bedroom to clean up.

"Grab your things," Mom said. Like roaches when the lights come on, we were all tripping over one another trying to get the heck out of Dodge before he came back into the kitchen to take us all out. Within seconds, we were across the parking lot and the door to our apartment was closing behind us.

But then, with fear in my eyes and my heart, I was directed to go back across the street and into the lion's den. Why, you ask? Well… something had been forgotten – more like someone had been forgotten. During the mad dash to safety everyone had assumed that one of the others had grabbed the baby out of her high chair. Wrong. Incorrect. False! With ultimate speed, I was in and out and back across the lot before I could think about what I had done.

Once again, red and blue lights were flashing right outside our front door. The cops walked my dad down the stairs of his apartment and put him in the back seat of the cruiser. I felt so scared and sad, all at the same time. Why did this keep happening? When was this madness ever going to end? As hard as I tried to be strong, the cries that came from the cruiser as they drove him away were just too much for me to take. My tears fell steadily, even when I could no longer hear the echoes of his voice calling my name.

The very next day, Dad came walking down the hill towards the apartment complex. This is how we found out that he had been released from police custody. I don't have to tell those of you who have dealt with law enforcement concerning domestic violence, but in a word... Pathetic!

The family dynamics then changed drastically. My parents' divorce became final, and Dad moved back home to Ohio. Things seem to have happened so fast that they are still something of a blur. One moment, it was me and my sisters with Mom. The next thing I knew, Mom and Dad made an agreement for my baby sister to go live with him. The reasoning behind this was financial on Mom's end and emotional on Dad's.

My role in all this was that he asked for one of us, and there was no way I was going. The fact that a choice was made to separate us girls still continues to cause discomfort among my family today.

The effect of divorce on a family can be devastating. Still, I believe that if there is evidence of physical or emotional abuse, then there is sufficient reason to dissolve the marriage for the sake of both the couple and the children. The effects of such turmoil can live forever in the minds of all involved. In turn, this tends to perpetuate a cycle of unhealthy relationship patterns. I know because I have witnessed it first-hand.

Mom was now on her third marriage, and my father was on his second. I had no complaints in relation to my step-parents. At home, life with my mom and step-dad, whom I call Pops, was pretty peaceful most of the time. Their relationship was solid, despite the turbulence that came with them getting involved while he was still married. But, as fathers go, he was a keeper. One of my fondest teenage memories in California was the day he showed up at the house, loaded us in the car and drove us down to San Diego for the day. We rode Malibu Go-Carts, visited Sea World and, on our return home, finished the night off at the drive-in movie theater. The relationship that he and I developed was very close, and remains so to this day.

I was excited to be starting High School. On the West Coast, it goes from grades nine to twelve. Making it even better, we lived in the Valley, which meant we would be attending a very nice high school. It sat atop this giant hill and had an open campus layout. To say it was way cool is an understatement. This excitement was short-lived, though. Because of the struggle with finances, Mom picked up and moved us back to Kans-ass!

The place reeked of feed yards and slaughtered meat. The locals called it "the smell of money" but, let's face it, it was literally the smell of cow *&^%. Even worse, I had tasted High School for five months, and now I was back in Junior High. Just shoot me now! Four months of that, then I could move up to the High School as a sophomore.

Family has always been important to me, no matter what. I tell friends that although my parents have more issues than some, they are still my parents, and I love them. It was not my choice who they were, nor is it my desire to banish them from my life. But so many times I wished and prayed that things could be different. With all the unrest and turmoil that seethed in our home, the moving around just made things that much worse. Moving here and there really sucked. Making friends wasn't difficult for me, but the leaving them behind was awful.

Over the years, people have commented that military families do it all the time. My response to that was, "Well, good for them, but my family isn't in the damned military!" My count may be off slightly (on the low end), but by the time I graduated in 1989, I had attended eleven different schools; five Elementary Schools (three up north, one Midwest, two West Coast), three Junior Highs (two West Coast, one Midwest) and two High Schools (one West Coast, one Midwest).

I only visited my dad and step-mom once, but the trip was extremely enjoyable. It was only the second time since my little sister had left that I had a chance to spend time with her and for us to be close. Our age gap was large, sixteen and six, but she stuck by my side the whole time. We played outside, I fixed her hair and we tried our best to fit as much in to our daily schedule as we could before I had to return home to Kansas.

I managed to make a couple of friends during that first year back in the Midwest. The three of us got really close and went pretty much everywhere together. I took my first real job, in the good old days of fast food restaurants. Life consisted of school, work and cruising Main Street. I knew that this was not where I wanted to spend the rest of my life, but after coming out of a year-long coma that was meant to punish my mother for moving me from sunshine to tumbleweeds, I met him. He was so cute, and he had this cool, laid-back swagger about him. He was, however, one of the local bad boys, but he was incredibly intelligent, despite his rough edges. His grades were impeccable and he was also on the high school wrestling team.

Imagine my surprise when he began working alongside me at the restaurant. Heaven! Life got even better when management put me in charge of producing the position chart and employee schedule. There were nights when I would purposely schedule a certain group of us to work the same hours so that we could hang out that night after work, at one of the local spots or the teen dance club 50 miles north in Dodge City.

It was the summer before my senior year, and I was now seventeen. As I was standing alone in the garage of my best friend's house pumping beer from the keg to celebrate her graduation, he walked in and began to strike up a conversation. Don't ask me what we talked about because I have no idea. All I know is that he was standing beside me one moment, and then the next we were lip-locked.

Okay, I don't want to come off as this unplucked flower experiencing her very first kiss. Truthfully, he was not. My "first" everything was with another young man, about two months earlier, who happened to be one of his best friends – here's how it went.

"Hurry up, we have to get on the road," my best friend said, as everyone was getting into the cars that would serve as our convoy out of town to go dancing in Dodge City. The music was awesome and several of us didn't waste any time running to the dance floor. Not sure who had been brave enough to sneak in the bottle of booze, but it was being passed around under the table until its contents were empty and everyone was feeling pretty good. Somehow on our way home, I ended up in the hatch of this guy's car making out while his friend was driving. No, I did not lose my virginity in the hatchback of that little, slightly crowded Z28. It was after we had gotten back to his house and snuck downstairs to his room. That's where "it" happened. Painfully, so I didn't see fireworks or hear trumpets playing. "It" was just over.

Anyway, all my attention for the next couple months was focused on him, and us. I was a complete goner; butterflies, fireworks the whole kit and caboodle. At the age of seventeen, I fell in love for the first time.

But just as quickly as it began, it ended. To say I was devastated was mild and by far the biggest understatement of the decade. How was it possible, to experience both love and heartache in such a short period of time? What I didn't know at the time was that, unlike me, he had already experienced the love bug at a very early age – fourteen, to be exact. Later, I learned that when he was in junior high school, a very friendly teacher of his became more than just his teacher. For two long years, this woman wined, dined and tutored him, in and out of the bedroom. Then without warning she did the inevitable and crushed his soul.

After our breakup, when I would see him walking through the halls at school, I did my best to remain invisible. Eventually, I was able to speak with him again without the fear of breaking into a million pieces. I discovered later that this would be the beginning of my draw and attraction to broken men.

My senior year of high school was not as pleasant as I hoped it would be, but I got through it and actually had more credits then I needed, so I was able to graduate earlier than the rest of my class. He and I developed what is now referred to as a "Friends with Benefits" relationship. For the next couple of years, I just sort of watched life go by. No matter where I was or what I was doing, I always found some way to make it back to him. Just like the song by Diana Ross says, "If you need me call me, no matter where you are, no matter how far." For two long years, I cried myself to sleep over this young man.

It wasn't until I actually moved away a few years later that I allowed another guy into my life, and even remotely close to my heart. No matter how hard we fight it or what we do to postpone it, eventually we all have to grow up. How that would happen for me was not even a blip on the radar when I was young and contemplating my future. It just goes to show, God has His own special plan for everyone.

CHAPTER 2
Combat Boots and Marriage

As we walked into the recruiting station in Texas (like I said, we moved around a lot), I wasn't as nervous as I thought I would be. After all, our country was at war. It might have had something to do with me not spending weeks contemplating the decision. Instead, I just woke up one morning and asked Pops to go with me while I enlisted. He had been in the military, as part of the Elite Special Forces, and served with the infamous 173rd, as had my dad as part of the 1st Calvary Regiment. Though in separate units, both made their contribution during the Vietnam War.

I intended to join the Air Force, but the staff had gone to lunch, so the Army side of the house was more than willing to step up and fill in. I made this choice at a time when I was unsure of my life's direction. Joining the military just made the most sense to me. I would have a steady paycheck, free food, a place to lay my head, travel the world, meet new people and see new things. Besides, that's what I had done all my life and, looking back, it seemed to be the natural next step.

We drove back to the house and walked through the door. Hey, Mom! Guess what? Not waiting for her to guess, I said, "I'm in the Army now." Pops and I were grinning and laughing, but there was nothing that looked like a smile on my mom's face. She was livid, and Pops caught holy heck that night for being my co-conspirator. It wasn't that she didn't want me to serve. She just didn't want me in the Army. She felt it more appropriate to enlist in the Air Force. But at the age of twenty, it was ultimately my decision. I had already lived on my own since graduating from high school when I was eighteen. My sister and I were roommates during those two years and I worked, and though it was only for a minimum wage, it was something to help contribute to the bills.

Well, once the dust settled, and it was evident that I would soon be leaving the nest for good, time just zoomed by. I fondly recall filling out paperwork and having to walk like a duck, and stuff myself with bananas, peanut butter sandwiches and soda to get me to the minimum weight required to enter (even with an additional waiver for the other four pounds I lacked). I'd always been on the small side of things and teetered between 79 and 82 pounds on the scale. When friends and family heard of my impending departure, the consensus was, "She's so tiny, there's no way she will be able to keep up with everyone or carry all the equipment that's required." Well, I would show everyone just how strong I was and prove them all wrong. On November 20, 1990, without hesitation or reservation, I raised my hand, said good-bye to my family, and boarded a plane headed for the East Coast.

Before I go any further, let me explain a few things about myself that I feel are relevant to the experience on which I was about to embark. Growing up had its good times and bad times. My big sister was three years older than me, so she had to deal with my pestering and whining for many years. I've been told by my family that I was an ornery something. Apparently, I was somewhat of a leg-hugger, and would bite the occasional kid that tried to come up on the porch and invade my space. I was nick-named "wild child" by a friend of the family, and people still mock my singing dirty little sassy songs way back when. No doubt this behavior can be attributed to the fact that I was the baby for ten years until my parents had my little sister.

Let it be said right now that my little sister was the prettiest little baby girl! When she came home from the hospital, both my parents had the flu, so my older sister took care of the new bundle until Mom and Dad got better.

Even with all the dysfunction, I managed to maintain a pretty good sense of who I was up until around seventh grade. Now all these years later I look back and realize that those middle school years are hell for most kids, and that being young and stupid is just a natural part of growing up. But coupled with my family dynamics, it had a major effect on my self-esteem, my self-image and my self-worth. Things like, my hair was too short, my skin was too dark, or I was way too skinny. When puberty – or in my case lack thereof – hit, it seemed I was in the running for President of the Itty Bitty Titty Committee Club. My sense of style was non-existent and my face was pimply with a splotchy complexion. By seventh grade, I had lost the spunk for which I was known as a happy-go-lucky child. That was until I stepped onto South Carolina soil.

Having done part of my growing up in the Midwest, I was very familiar with livestock transports, but I never dreamed that I would actually ride in one in a million years. A cattle truck… Seriously? This is an acceptable mode of transportation for people? Yes, indeed it was, and no one dared to say otherwise.

It wasn't long before I adjusted to the fact that all I needed to do was be where I was told to be and do what I was told to do. From the reception station to the basic barracks we went, bogged down with bags and equipment. The screams and fast pace of it all were frantic. I remember laying in my bunk that first night thinking, "What in the world have I gotten myself into?"

That feeling quickly changed as I became more and more comfortable with what the training was all about. It was like giving newly issued boots a fresh polish. There was really nothing wrong with the way they looked or functioned, but adding a bright new coat just enhanced their appeal and performance. I could feel the "I can't" and "It's too hard" attitude melting from my genetic make-up. The harder they pushed, the stronger I got. At one point, Papa Smurf and Robo Drill (nicknames we gave our drill sergeants) showed me the utmost respect for my apparent desire to "be all that I could be," that is, while still maintaining something of a class clown demeanor. They had me doing push-ups every time I turned around, but they also gave me extra dessert to help beef me up a little bit. The combination of the two worked because at the end of those eight long weeks, I was in the best shape of my life. Weighing in at one hundred pounds, man, I had a butt, legs, arms and killer abs. I must say though, my abs are still pretty sweet today.

Advanced Individual Training (AIT) was similar, but with a little more freedom to move around.

My physical strength increased, placing me in the only female slot running with the guys. Class time consisted of us typing for speed. Day in and day out, we pecked away at the computer, and it paid off as I was awarded the status of Honor Grad for my class.

The nice thing about AIT was the off-post passes given to us each weekend. As long as we did what we were supposed to during the week, we were free to wander the streets of Jacksonville, South Carolina, and boy did we ever! Come Saturday mornings, hotel reservations were already made, and we were off and running. Like so many before me, I too had a boyfriend during this phase of training. He was very sweet, and we even spoke of marriage, but after graduation he went to Indiana and me to Fort Bragg, North Carolina. Sure, we tried to make it work for a while, to no avail. Our relationship ended three short months after we finished AIT. It didn't help that when I went home on leave after training, I spent some time with my high school sweetie. All the old feelings were still there.

Now, life in the Army was not bad at all: three squares a day and a free place to live. Moving into the barracks was different, to say the least. It was designed to be a four-man room, but there were only three of us in there, which was nice. What I didn't expect was to have my two roommates' boyfriends in there with them most of the time. I was not the type to complain, so I just dealt with it.

The first six months at Bragg were a blast, meeting all the new people, really being out on my own, and the partying that goes along with being new to the military. It became routine for a group of us to drive to neighboring Pope Air Force Base for drinking and dancing every weekend. It was nicer and much safer than the enlisted club on Fort Bragg, affectionately known as "The Stab and Jab". We figured it was better to be safe than sorry. Though how safe, or rather how smart, was it for us to risk driving across post to take part in underage drinking, and then to travel back across post while intoxicated? Oh, to be young and stupid!

On the work front, things were coming together quite nicely. I was becoming more proficient at my job, which was a feat considering, that our syllabus at school did not include processing awards, personnel actions, promotions or evaluations. My physical work location was in the S-1 shop at the brigade level, which consisted of five subordinate battalions that operated below us. The unit I was in did not have the best reputation on post and surprisingly, I hear it still has a lot of the same issues today. I celebrated my twenty-first birthday at Chi Chi's, a Mexican restaurant not far from post. This marked my first legal consumption of alcohol, as well as being a month shy of my first year of military service.

Life was on track now, and I realized that for me, the Army was a perfect fit. Over the next few months, my high school sweetie and I reconnected and were corresponding on a regular basis. Now, the interesting thing that you must know about this relationship was that while I was off establishing a new life, he was finishing up his first stint in rehab, and I was there to encourage and help him through the process. I knew for years that he had a dependency on alcohol, but I didn't care. It never deterred my quest for him in the slightest. I loved him, and everything was going to be all right.

At Christmas 1991, I got a shiny little package in the mail from him. Without a second thought, I said "Yes". Within two months he had completed his required stay at a half-way house, after leaving rehab in

Kansas. He packed his bags and hopped a bus heading for North Carolina. As a Private First Class, my paychecks were small, as you would expect. Neither one of us had a car, nor did he have a job, which made my supervisor very reluctant to sign my request to live off post. Lo and behold, by February of 1992 he and I had made our cohabitation official. Life was great, and we were so happy. All we had was this little, ratty single-wide trailer, older than the both of us put together. I can still remember being unable to buy oil for heat, so we would hibernate in the back bedroom with every blanket we owned. To be young and in love… Yeah!

The friendship we had developed in high school just seemed to get stronger. One of the sweet things that we shared on those cold nights was the warmth of our bodies, and his request for me to sing to him, which I did without pause. He always liked the sound of my voice and the smile it put on his face made me feel good. In the first four months he was there, the closeness we shared was like none I had every felt. We were truly becoming one. Maybe it was because we had very little money to go out and do different things, or maybe it was because it was just us, with no family around to speak of. We were all we had and being holed up in our little abode gave us time to really get to know each other and spend lots of quality time together.

Well, the date was set. We were to be married on July fourth, 1992. I was so excited. Two of my good friends were going to be our witnesses. All was going according to plan until the night before our wedding. By this time, I had finally purchased a little 1980 Honda Prelude. It was a dreadful brown thing, minus heat and air conditioning. He had found a job in the next town over, working at a turkey plant. Gross, but it paid the bills, and it allowed him to make a few new friends. He and these new friends decided to have a boys' night out, pronounced "bachelor party". They assured me they would take care of him and get him back safe and sound for the wedding the following day.

By one o'clock in the morning he hadn't returned home, and I was starting to get worried. I couldn't sleep, and every sound was amplified in the trailer. Something was wrong – I could feel it. Just then, the phone rang, and on the other end was my soon-to-be mother-in-law. I could hear the nervousness in her voice as she questioned me on the whereabouts of her son, while at the same time telling me that she had received a call from him, stating that he'd been taken to jail. In a drunken haze the only number in his mental rolodex was his moms. Now it was freak-out time.

After countless phone calls and hours of missed sleep, I was able to gather the details of the evening that preceded his incarceration. Keeping it short, those friends were not good friends at all, and once he passed out, they put him in the car outside the bar... with the keys in the ignition. This is why I will always believe that over-indulgence in alcohol is one of the greatest diseases in our country. Also, if you recall, he had been dry and sober for the previous eight months. Anyway, when he woke up, still inebriated, he decided to drive himself home. Well, as you can surmise, he didn't make it. As a matter of fact, he visited a few road signs before arriving at his final destination... the ditch. If you would like to keep track, that was car number one.

The next day I was finally able to go visit him at the jailhouse. In his splendor, he sported a wonderful orange jumpsuit along with a shiny new black eye. He looked pitiful but, instead of running in the other direction, I told him that I wouldn't be able to get him out until the next day and that his bond was one thousand dollars. Now you may laugh, shake your head or look at me like I have snot running down my nose, as the magistrate did when I showed up the next day to pay the bond at ten o'clock, then returned with him and our two witnesses only four hours later – to be married.

It wasn't long before the reality of marriage, and the responsibilities that came along with it, sunk in. Once again, he fell off the wagon in a really bad way. It was a Friday night, and my sergeant from work was having a cookout at her house. I told him he could come, but if he did, he had to watch his drinking. His response was, "Fine, I just won't go then."

While I was there, without him, mind you, he called no less than six or seven times, begging me to come home. I was not ready to go home. He was just going to have to suck it up and wait. The last call he made was to inform me that he had taken a partial bottle of aspirin, drunk all of the Nyquil, and whatever else he could get his hands on there in the house. I had refused to buy him anything to drink before I left for the party, so now he was trying to punish me for leaving him home alone and dry.

Upon my return home the next morning, I found him pale, and curled up in the corner of the bathroom. Scared of what lay before me, I quickly got him to the car and took him straight to Womack Medical Center, on post. Here I am, a mere Private First Class newly married, bringing my sick husband to the emergency room to have his stomach pumped. I was nervous, embarrassed, scared and angry all at the same time. If he had died, I would have brought him back to life so I could kill him myself. How was I going to explain this one to my chain of command? Luckily, they were accommodating and gave me the time I needed to get him home and back on his feet.

Around this time, the relationship between my father and I had turned a corner and he had brought my sister down from Ohio to visit us in North Carolina. There was still some mending to be done, but I was thankful that my younger sister and I were able to spend more time getting to know each other. She was now twelve years old and had a lot more personality then she had the time I had visited her at age six.

Things settled down for us after that. My husband climbed back on the wagon and got a better job, and I got promoted to Specialist. What a year it had been for us! With things progressing well, we moved out of the trailer and into this adorable little one-bedroom mushroom house across town. I bought us a new car, and he had just finished up school to acquire his Certified Nursing Assistant license. For the next couple years, things were up and down, but we managed to get through whatever was thrown at us. All the while he was asking me to have a baby. Yeah, no!

We were doing well to take care of ourselves, let alone a baby.

Four years into marriage, I had just completed the Primary Leadership Development Course (PLDC) to advance to the rank of Sergeant, while working a part-time job at night, selling jewelry to keep myself busy. He was working as a mortgage broker and going to college full-time, pursuing a business degree. Still leery about the whole baby idea, I decided to take some leave to go visit family and friends back home. He had class and a busy work schedule, so he stayed behind for this trip.

Color me pink as my maternal instincts kicked in while watching all my friends doting over their little bundles of joy. Two weeks into the trip I stopped taking the birth control pills I had been on since the age of fifteen. Yes, fifteen. It's a family tradition that I am proud to say still lives on. No teenage mothers for this crew. Once I returned home from my trip, little did he know, but it was on and poppin'! I can tell you the exact day my daughter was conceived, January 28, 1994. Don't ask me how; just take my word for it.

Now, the story of how I found out that I was actually pregnant was sad and sweet. News came that my uncle had lost his fight against lung cancer. I had just been home two months prior and was able to spend time with him while he was still up and moving around. Once again, I left for home to attend the funeral without my husband because of the short notice. My flight back to Bragg was rough and choppy, causing my stomach to pray for a quick landing. It was not unusual for me to have tummy issues during a flight, but this was worse than usual. I blamed the crop duster used to transport me between Charlotte and Fayetteville.

The airplane finally touched down, and it felt so good to be on the ground. After picking up my bags, I headed to the door to see if he was there waiting to pick me up. To my surprise he was nowhere to be found. He didn't answer the phone at the house, so now I was stuck at the airport without a ride home. Thankfully, my girlfriend was home and said that she would come pick me up. My mind was racing a thousand miles per hour now, wondering where in the world he could be.

Eventually, we pulled up to the house, got out the car and headed up to the door. She happened to look back for whatever reason, and then asked me, "What's wrong with the front of your car?" You will not believe what I saw upon closer inspection of the vehicle. At the time, I had a cute little silver Honda Civic, which I got after trading in the Prelude and he had recently traded in his 6 month old motorcycle for a new Honda Accord. Well, the Accord was missing a prominent part of its body – the front bumper. That was car number two. The bumper had been carefully placed inside of the car.

Beyond upset at this point, I walked back to the house to find the front door wide open, lights on, money from his pay check spread all over the table, and him missing in action.

As I began to unpack and settle back in from the trip, I heard him walk through the door and wander upstairs to the bedroom where I was.

"So, what happened to the car?" I said. "And thanks for picking me up from the airport."

Do you know this nut actually had the nerve to get lippy with me. "I don't understand what happened," he said. "It wasn't my fault. And I wasn't even the one driving the car."

It was as if providing me with that tidbit of information was going to make it all right. At one point in the conversation, he really started feeling himself because, without warning, he picked up the iron from the ironing board and threw it against the wall. Fear instantly appeared on his face because he knew I would have him hemmed up for doing something so stupid. In my calm wifely voice, I instructed him to put on his shoes and coat, walk his silly self over to the Post Exchange, and buy a new iron because he needed to get his clothes ready for work the next day. With his tail between his legs, he did as he was told, and we went on with the rest of our evening.

Later that week I was still feeling a little funny, so instead of blowing it off I decided to pee on a stick. I left work at lunchtime, stopped by the store for a test, picked up a slice of pizza and then proceeded home to learn the results.

It didn't seem real at first. I sat there and looked at that little piece of plastic sitting on the edge of the bathtub with a dark pink line flashing through it. The pizza I bought didn't seem as appetizing as it did before, and my heart was beating steady and swiftly. I quickly ran next door to my girlfriend's house and gave her the news. She was so excited for me. Her daughter was about to turn a year old, so she knew exactly how I felt. As I drove back to work, a million things were going through my head. "Oh my God, I'm pregnant!" "I am actually going to have a baby."

That night when my husband got home from work, and I popped the news to him. He didn't believe me. After years of me shooting down his requests to conceive, he thought I was joking. Laughing, I told him that I was serious and that it was real.

"Until I see a medical slip from your doctor, I won't believe it," he countered.

His futile attempts to knock me up in the past had him skeptical about the truth of my situation. Therefore, without delay I went to visit the doctor the next morning and brought home the proof he'd requested. You should have seen the joy and excitement on his face.

He kept repeating, "We're going to have a baby. I can't believe you are finally having my baby." He was so happy. I knew he wanted a child desperately, and though I was a little nervous, I was happy to be having his baby too.

As you would expect, the news spread like wildfire. Family, friends and random acquaintances were all in the know that we were to be expecting our own little bundle of joy within the year.

My mom's reaction was bittersweet at first. Although I was twenty-four years old, four years into my marriage and serving my country in the United States Army, she feared for my health during the pregnancy. Her concern did have some legitimacy, because just a year earlier, after a few medical procedures, we had found out that I only had one kidney. It seems I was just born that way. True, you only need one to survive, but as we came to find out, pregnancy can put a major strain on a woman's kidneys, especially during the final trimester. We provided all of this pertinent information to my doctor during my initial visit. As a result, I was put in the high-risk category and treated very well by the medical staff at Womack Army Medical Center.

The pregnancy progressed very well. I'm growing my wonderful baby belly, eating fresh-picked strawberries, Fazoli's cheese cake and bread sticks, and making multiple trips per week to Red Lobster. I continued working, though now I made it out of the trenches and moved up to the higher headquarters of my command. My sweetie was still in school and also working fast and furious on an operating manual that would be implemented and used as the main training tool for his company. It appeared from the outside that all was well in our household.

But the closer it got to my due date, the more out of whack things became. He was off the wagon again and on a steady downward spiral. I was due to deliver our precious cargo on the 30th of October and something had to give. So, we sat down one evening, had a serious talk and by the middle of September, we were on the road to Wilmington, North Carolina, where he voluntarily checked himself into substance abuse treatment for the second time. At eight months pregnant, I well recall making the drive a couple times to see him at the facility. They recommended that his stint be longer, but after only two weeks, he checked himself out and returned home clean and sober.

Actually the timing couldn't have been better. We were able to celebrate my twenty-fifth birthday together, and then exactly one week later I had a routine doctor's appointment at the hospital. Just as in the weeks prior, I checked into the fourth floor where they performed the stress test on my belly. This consisted of them strapping a belt-like device around my stomach that had little metal buttons sticking out of it. Then, they would proceed to tap on the little metal buttons with a spoon. Hey, gotta love modern medicine. Well, on this particular day, the tapping failed to produce any movement from the baby. Usually it would start doing the tango, but not today.

Then, they made me go into another room where a nurse and an ultrasound technician lathered me up with the blue goo and took a look at what was going on inside. After a few twists and turns of the wand along with some secret spoken words, in walked the doctor. "How would you feel about having a baby tonight"? The question was put to me as if they were asking whether I'd like the tuna or the salmon. Ha ha!

The doctor's demeanor really put me at ease as she explained the reasoning behind her decision to induce my labor. It turned out that the baby had run out of room to grow, decreasing the amount of fluid that was required to sustain life in the womb. See? We learn something new every day.

I had only gained twenty pounds during my pregnancy. I started at ninety-eight, and on that day, I checked in at one hundred eighteen. Another question the doc asked is whether I knew the baby's sex and, if not, whether I wanted to. My eyes got real wide because we did not know our baby's sex. We just knew that it was coming and no matter what it was, we were blessed. So I paused for a moment and said, "Sure." She sweetly replied, "I hope you've got some pink paint." I could hardly believe it… We were going to have a beautiful baby girl!

Before settling into my room, they gave me a phone so that I could call my husband and let him know the new game plan. He immediately closed up shop and headed straight to the hospital. I told him it would be a while before things got moving, so to stop by the house for my bag and a few other things. Before I knew it, he was standing in front of me, panting as if he had just completed a marathon. He was so sweet though, very attentive and super excited. Once they hooked me up to all the proper machines and devices, I finally convinced him that it would be okay if he went home and got the items we needed. It wasn't like he had to drive all the way across town. We lived right on post, approximately two miles from the hospital.

He quickly returned and was relieved to find me just as he had left me. It was seven o'clock in the evening when the doctor ordered my Pitocin drip to induce labor. Most of our night consisted of watching

TV, and the clock, and him with that darn video camera. It seemed like he documented every hour, on the hour. "Okay," he would say, "this is the machine that monitors the contractions," followed by, "See, one's coming right now." Keeping me warm and comfortable was his sole mission. I could not have asked for a better partner with whom to experience this. I remember waking early that next morning to find him asleep on the floor, his head propped on a bag right next to my bed. Nothing could ever compare to that image of him not wanting to leave my side. That act alone told me there could never be any doubt that this man truly loved me. No matter what would come after this, I would always be able to say that I've felt, touched, breathed and experienced true love in my lifetime.

Our love would soon be tested, though, as the induction medicine began to kick in and I wanted drugs. Of, course it was much too soon, but I never imagined how painful it would be. Call me a wimp, but I had never even experienced menstrual cramps, so I was clueless.

The hands on the clock are moving so slow, and I am ready to have this little person out of me. Let the fun begin. It's now ten in the morning, and I finally received my epidural – better, but not perfect. I had no idea that this was not an exact science, but as I wait to feel the full effects of the medication, I realize that it has only worked on the right side of my body, and I can still feel all of the pain on my left. I am aggravated, and the saga continues.

Hours have passed, and nothing. No dilation, no water breakage, nothing. This calls for an intervention by the doctor. He has to come in and break my water. Ouch! I begin to cry at this point, but am quickly comforted by my husband telling me that everything is going to be all right. Little do we know that, although this will turn out to be true in the end, the fun has only just begun. After a few hours of cervical checks, I'm ready to go. Everyone is scurrying around prepping me for the delivery room. My sweetie is in his blue gown and booties while I look like the bride of Frankenstein, hair a total mess, glasses still on and oxygen strapped to my face. Away we go, down the hall.

It doesn't get off to a good start in the delivery room as the anesthesiologist and I exchange unkind words because of the pain I still feel on my left side, causing me to yelp upon initial contact for my episiotomy. For all those who don't know, an episiotomy is when a sharp metal scalpel is used to make a slit on each side of the vagina, to decrease the chance of ripping as the baby comes through the birth canal. Aw... what a pretty picture. While I am professionally diverted by the cool head of my doctor, he quickly administers a local anesthetic, also known as a saddle block. I can't even begin to explain the expression on my face when I see the instrument set to deliver that numbing potion, but I am thankful for its results. Tired and worn, I so want this to hurry up. I push, yet nothing is happening. This lazy little girl is not ready to come out!

Noticing that I am on the verge of exhaustion, the doctor softly says, "If you can give me one more big push, I promise I will get her out." True to his word, he grabs the forceps. I push, he pulls, I rip, and there she is. October 11, 1995 at 5:43pm marks the exact time I officially become a mother. She is 5 lbs. 4 oz. and 19 inches long. There aren't enough words in the English dictionary to describe the miracle that God has blessed us with this day.

My initial visit with her is brief as the doctor needs to tend to my next medical procedure. Two hours and fifty-six stitches later, I am in my room when they bring me this tightly wound cocoon.

"You did it, Mommy," are the first words out of my husband's mouth when he sits beside me on the bed as I hold our daughter in my arms. We should all be lucky enough to bathe in a euphoric moment such as this.

Becoming a parent changed me in a lot of ways. For so long, it had all been about me; what I wanted, what I needed. Suddenly, there was this little person that would need me to be all things to her until she became old enough to tackle the world alone. My potty mouth vanished, at once. The selfish ways that had followed me since childhood began to disappear. I knew from the moment I saw her that I wanted to be the best mother I could be. As a matter of policy, a female soldier gets six weeks off after having a baby, and I took full advantage of this luxury. It helped tremendously to have my mother there to help for the first two weeks. Not only did she tend to the baby, but she was able to assist me in healing from the whole delivery ordeal.

The first six months seemed to fly right by, from the first bottle of cereal to the piercing of her ears at three months. Our first Christmas as a family of three was massive. We went and had a real tree chopped down. I spared no expense on ornaments and gifts. Though only three months old, she had presents spilling out from under the tree. I had never taken so many pictures in my life. We went to the photo studio to have her picture taken every month. Who knew that it would result in her being such a ham, now?

Easter was about to arrive, and that would mark the start of a new adventure. We prepared for our first family photo.

The significance of this was that my husband's employment status had changed. Because of a conflict within his agency, he quit his job and was unable to work as a broker in the state of North Carolina for a year. This prompted the bright idea to move to Oklahoma, closer to family, and to get work there. The major downside of this was that I still had six more months left in the Army. I had to submit paperwork to get out early for reasons of family hardship. Since it was going to take a couple months to complete this process, we agreed that the baby would go forward with him, where he would have help and support from our families.

April 1996, I waved good-bye to my family as they drove away without me. It was one of the hardest things I've ever done in my life, but that kept me focused on doing what I needed to do to get to them as soon as I could. By May 31st my paperwork was finally complete. I packed up the house, cleared government quarters, and hopped in my rented Penske truck and headed west to reunite with my family.

After two days of driving, there was only one minor glitch. I was towing my car, so backing up was pretty difficult. Well, I made a miscalculation at a hotel where I was staying and ended up in a ditch. It could have happened to anyone. I simply made a phone call and the tow truck pulled me out, pronto. It just gave me a cool story to tell when I finally arrived at the house.

It felt so good to see my baby girl again. By getting out of the service with an honorable discharge, I was entitled to receive unemployment benefits for six months, which gave me time to spend with her while putting out feelers for work. Never did I imagine that it would be so difficult to find a job, but then again, I was in Stillwater, Oklahoma. There we sat, four months after the move. Neither one of us had a job, but the bills still needed to be paid. Stress and tension began to build, and he was drinking again. We began drifting further and further apart.

In November of that same year, I told him that I wanted out. I loved him, I truly did, but I was tired. It had become so hard to keep it all together. His alcoholism had finally taken its toll on me. With the stress and the worry of it all, I had been diagnosed with acid reflux. The symptoms and doctor's visits had been increasing over the past two years. After drinking nasty concoctions and being jolted around on a sterile x-ray machine, having scopes placed down my throat and tubes up my nose, I was finally prescribed a medication that would ease some of the discomfort associated with the illness. I put all my belongings in storage and moved in with my parents. They only had a little two-bedroom apartment on the university campus, so I knew that I would have to make other arrangements for my daughter and me quickly.

Still, with no job and very few options, I decided to spend one night in a shelter while my parents kept my daughter. This was the only way to get expedited housing for my daughter and me. I lay in that bed alone and in the dark, crying and asking myself how I had gotten to this point. As hard as it was, I would have run through fire if it meant that she would have a roof over her head. The next day I checked out and was given a voucher to rent an apartment for twenty dollars a month. I also received daycare assistance, food stamps and Medicaid. Thankfully, my mom's boss was able to put in a good word for me at the college, and I was offered a job at the university. My husband had also started working, and it seemed we were both getting back on our feet. It was crazy how just one short year earlier, I had experienced a miracle, but at this point my faith was being tested.

While I was climbing out of the hole that I had put myself in, my husband took a turn for the worse and needed help like never before. Racking my brain for a solution, I reached out to the mortgage company that he had worked for back on the East Coast and told them he needed to come home. A week later they had arranged for his return trip to North Carolina. They gave him a job, a place to stay and a car to drive.

As he settled back into his familiar environment, I informed him that he also needed to go to an attorney and file divorce papers. It may sound cruel but, I was so tired and my health had really started to suffer from all the angst and anxiety of his drinking and our failing relationship. I slept sitting up over many nights because the act of lying down was just too painful. He begged me to reconsider, but I just needed out. I told him that he would be able to see our daughter anytime he wanted and that all of the strict, legal mumbo jumbo would not dictate how we raised our child.

Well, after going back and forth with him about where our lives were, and what we needed to do one more time in order for things to work, I decided to move back to North Carolina and give it one last try.

I know what you are thinking, but he was the father of my child. I had loved this man since I was sixteen years old! In September of 1997, I packed up the car, the little one, and I hit the road east. Now, you must know that even though I'd agreed to give it another shot, I was still adamant about him continuing with our divorce proceedings.

Once we got back in North Carolina, the house where he was living belonged to a man who was uncomfortable with me living there because of the color of my skin, so we did some house hunting and settled into a nice, quiet little neighborhood in the town of

Hope Mills. I recall us playing outside in the driveway with our daughter one day when the mailman showed up with a large manila envelope. Unaware of its contents, I opened it, and it was official. We were actually divorced, per the state of North Carolina. We sort of stared at each other for a moment, embraced and instantly filed the papers away.

Things were going pretty good for us again, for a while. Since his return, his business partner and he had worked tirelessly to form their own company, with the backing of a very prominent businessman in town. Due to tenacity and ambition, no longer would there be a Wachovia building, but rather the Systel building. His mark in the business world had come to fruition. Shortly thereafter, he was sitting in a corner office on the penthouse level of the largest building in downtown Fayetteville. Not only was he Vice President, but he created the company's policies and procedures. I was so proud of him. Here beside me was this handsome, young, twenty-five-year-old man from Kansas sitting on top of the world. Through all the ups and downs, ins and outs, he had made it.

Despite all the success around us, home was not as cozy as everyone perceived it to be. He never missed work, but the drinking and other recreational party favors in which he partook woke me back up. We had finally reached the end of our journey. It was time to bow out gracefully. I left the pretty, two-story home, the nice Mercedes that sat in the driveway and the income that was coming in – all of it. I took my income tax money, bought myself a little hooptie, found a little one-bedroom duplex nearby and started working at a car dealership in town.

The relationship had fizzled about a month before I actually moved, and I was well aware that he had started seeing a young lady with whom he worked.

So, the day after I moved out, he was moving her in. It stung a bit at first, but within a couple of weeks, I was back at his house talking to her about my expectations since she was going to be in my daughter's life. She was this sweet, young, twenty-one or twenty-two year old, little, blonde Barbie-doll type. I explained to her that when I left, I had taken very few of my belongings due to the size of my new place, and the one essential thing I needed access to was the washer and dryer. With a two year old, laundry was a constant, and I refused to pay a Laundromat as long as I was caring for our child. So, each week I would be dropping by to wash clothes. We also discussed the times when she would actually be the one "taking care" of my daughter because of his after-work habits. All was understood, and there were no problems between the two of us.

It wasn't long before the fun of playing house turned into reality for her. Sitting at my desk one day at work, I received a phone call from none other than the girlfriend, obviously upset and confused. You see, people thought I was a fool for walking away from such a sweet, cool hard-working guy. Now, there she was, asking if he had ever hit me. Had he ever done this or that, and "he drinks so much". All I could say to her was, "No. He never dared to hit me," and that I was sorry, but the rest she would have to deal with because it was no longer my problem. In his defense, he was never a violent man; silly when intoxicated, but never mean. Though certain personalities can clash, and when you add alcohol to the mix it can get ugly. From what I was told, they were having an argument and she slapped him and he slapped her back. Wrong, but not my problem.

I had started going out again, and am not ashamed to admit that I had found a little cutie that would meet my girlfriend and me at the club each weekend and heat me up on the dance floor, then take me home. Being grown and single, I could do whatever it was I wanted. It was weird at first because my ex-husband had been the only one for so long, but I quickly adapted and just decided to allow myself a little bit of fun. The car business had run its course with me, so I got back to what I knew and began working for the title division of a bank. It was now time to start living life again.

CHAPTER 3 Part 1
The Lost Years

Time sure seems to fly when things are going well in life. Living with my daughter and a roommate in a bigger, nicer place, new job and a fresh outlook, I met The Rebound. This was a relationship that didn't involve much thought before diving in. It had been eight months since the divorce and five months from the day I moved out. Feeling that it was time to put myself back in the game, I posted a "personals" ad in the newspaper (this was during the pre-internet era). I was never the type to approach some random bloke while out and about, nor did I possess the patience to just sit around waiting for him to come to me, so I used what means were available.

After a few phone calls, this guy and I decided to meet face-to-face. It was a pleasant first date. We took a walk down by the lake, laughed and talked while feeding the ducks. Before saying goodnight for the evening, we decided to go out again the next day.

A little background information on this fellow: he had once served in the Army. I can't remember the number of years, but upon his exit from the military he started driving trucks, long-haul. He had a nice, clean truck and owned a home in a nearby neighborhood. The Rebound had also been married with five children, two biological and three stepchildren. That said, I figured any man that was willing to take on a woman with three children had to be a pretty stand-up guy.

The location of our next meeting was a little different. It was down the street from his house at the Laundromat. He explained to me that he was washing his own clothes because he and his wife were not divorced yet, but separated. Though still living in the same house, it was merely for financial reasons. Against my better judgment, I didn't run. Once he finished his clothes he suggested dinner, but first he would need to go drop off his things at the house. What happened next is just like watching one of those bad B-rated horror movies, predictable and downright tacky. We pulled into the driveway; he jumped out and calmly walked through the front door. I was unaware that his wife was looking outside and saw me in the truck. This was not good for him, at all.

Next thing I saw was him bolting from the porch with her right on his butt. They scrapped for a bit in the yard and in the process, she ripped the chain off his neck. Trying to escape the scene while at the same time defending himself from her flails, he finally managed to break free and jump in the truck. At this point, I was in complete shock as to what had just happened but really didn't have time to speak because as fast as he entered the vehicle we were backing out of the driveway and she gave chase behind us. Up the street, down the street, through neighborhoods, downtown, across town, no matter his direction she was on his tail. This went on for about an hour before he was finally able to lose her. The truck came to a stop, and it was evident the coast was clear.

"Question: What in the H#$% was that all about... and is it going to follow me to my house?"

At this point a normal person would have politely said farewell and bid him adieu. Nope. Not me. I told him that it would all be okay and invited him to stay at my house. You don't have to say it. (Broken men, remember.) I already know, but hindsight is 20/20.

Over the next several weeks, his real situation became a little clearer to me. After numerous phone calls to my house and tantrums left on the answering machine, some of the truth began to come out, as it always does. The fact was, his wife had been dating someone, but when he decided to do the same, it pissed her off. It was one of those, "I don't want him anymore, but don't want to see him with anyone else either" scenarios.

I also had a glimpse of that from my ex around the same time. Although still with his girlfriend, he liked to check in on me every now and then. One night he stopped by the house without calling and found our daughter there with my roommate while I was out on a date. A little monkey jumped on his back, and he felt it necessary to curse me out for leaving her with a stranger. We both knew that wasn't what got his panties in a bunch. It was the fact that I had also moved on. But, for some reason, he had to take it to another level.

Before leaving my house, he kindly removed the hoses from my distributor cap. Hah! Very funny right? Well the joke was on him because, ironically, his company and mine did business together on a regular basis. He was into brokering mortgages and my bank supplied the title insurance to complete the deal. The next day, pretending to be on an official call, he got patched through to my line. Laughing, he asked me how my trip into work went that morning. Instead of going through the phone and ripping his tongue out, I just chuckled and told him it was not nice to mess with a woman's livelihood. Then I hung up the phone.

Only a select few knew of all the things that he and I went through. To help him get back on his feet after we split, I agreed to minimal child support; one hundred fifty dollars per month, to be exact. Our arrangement was that if I needed more money, all I would have to do is stop by the office and he would write me a check. So after three years of being nice, this little incident caused me to pick up the phone and have his financial records reevaluated by the state of Oklahoma (thankfully I didn't switch it over to North

Carolina because there, a child could go hungry waiting for it to be enforced). Let's just say that during his next phone call to me, he was not laughing.

Now, it wasn't long before things calmed down for me and The Rebound. His wife started letting him see his children again, and they were allowed to come over for visits. She also moved out of the marital home. My lease was about to be up, and with my roommate moving out, I agreed to his suggestion of us moving into his old house. Right before the move, we learned that the mortgage had fallen behind and would need to be caught up. Since it was his property, he made the necessary arrangements and got things back in line with the payments. I knew that I would be contributing to the household, but at the time, my income was once again shallow. I had decided to quit my job at the bank to enroll in college, full-time. I had my GI Bill and child support, so I was still able to help out with some of the bills.

Well, I was warned not to freak when I got to the house to look around because the damage was extensive. That didn't prepare me for how absolutely gross it was in that place! The house had been severely neglected. The walls, doors and appliances were broken. The carpets and floors where terribly stained and a forest was growing in the front and back yard. His wife and five kids had been living in that squalor. Not from lack of money, but from a lack of concern for the property.

The Rebound had been in an accident at work, so they paid him a nice settlement that allowed us to go in, roll up our sleeves and completely clean house. This was my first experience with a home remodel. We installed closet units, hung doors, spackled walls, painted, changed electric receptacles and light fixtures, and revamped the entire kitchen with new appliances and pretty navy blue tile floors.

It was 1999 and, even though I had gone through so much with The Rebound, I always knew this was not a man I wanted to marry. By the spring of 2000, he knew it too. I was still in school but had adjusted to the routine of school and motherhood, so I decided to go back to work. The job I took was actually pretty cool. Though I was only an Assistant Gift Shop Manager, what made it great was that I worked for the Airborne and Special Operations Museum in downtown Fayetteville. For one thing, when I was active duty, I was a part of the Special Operations Command. Secondly, this place was still naked when a lot of us came on board.

My job was not just to sell things. I hired and trained our retail staff, including one special lady with whom I am still very good friends with today. I met with vendors who specialized in military memorabilia, and decided what would be stocked and what wouldn't. With the museum logo in hand, I ventured out to the screen printers on my own and generated the design for our grand opening shirts. We also met with local jewelers for special pieces to fill our cases. The manager and I did business with a well-known clothing distributor right outside of town that would provide most of our souvenir gear.

There were clothes, music, art, books, toys, jewelry, glassware and so much other cool stuff, and these were just the things in the gift shop. The artifacts donated and created by the staff of the museum were treasures in themselves. The museum also had a movie room and a simulator. The community support was fantastic, which brought about school tours, holiday parties and official events. The grand opening boasted names such as Ross Perrot and a jump-in by the Army's prestigious Golden Knights. You may or may not be able to tell, but I was very honored and proud to have been a part of its beginning.

With job satisfaction, school going well and my baby girl accepted into the Pre-K program, the only thing left to do was end my expired relationship with The Rebound. I was able to do this because in the summer of two thousand, my family moved from Oklahoma to North Carolina for a change of scenery and to be closer to the baby and me. Upon arrival, my sister found and closed on a house that would fit the whole clan. It was her and my nephew, Mom and Pop, along with my little one and me.

With The Rebound's divorce final, he tried sticking around for a while, but I told him that he needed to move on. Oh yeah, his truck had been repossessed a few weeks earlier because when I thought he was paying bills, he wasn't. So, to give him a fresh start I gave him my little hooptie so that he could get to and from work. Finally, I retired The Rebound.

In August 2000, I turned my focus on school, work and my daughter. There was little time for anything else. It felt good to take a break from being in a relationship for a while. I was really happy just being me. The little one, now four, was about to start kindergarten. We had a blast shopping for required school supplies and those cute navy blue jumpers that were part of the student uniform. To my surprise, "Little Miss Independent" didn't want me to take her to school on the first day, but she generously granted permission for me to watch her walk with her cousin the one block it took to get there from our house. Being there when she got home from her first day was also beyond cool. She was beaming with joy while talking to me about all the things she did that day. For those parents who have experienced this... Priceless!

But life as we knew it was about to change.

Things had changed slightly for my ex-husband. He and his girlfriend had broken up, and he asked for some help moving into a smaller place closer to work. He was fortunate to find a cute apartment just a couple blocks from his job. After living there for a few weeks, he called me saying that he needed a ride home from the gym because he was just too tired to ride his bike back to the house. Don't rack your brain about why he was riding a bike instead of driving. Suspended license.

He had already wrecked the Mercedes once (ran into a railroad control box), but it could be fixed, and was. The next time, he wasn't as lucky. He hit a lady from behind, and that time it was totaled – carted away. Then he bought a brand-new candy apple red truck but was unable to drive it for a while. No worries, though. He knew I would help him out whenever I could.

When I arrived at the gym, I could tell that he didn't look well, but just figured he had over-exerted himself. I dropped him off at home and said I would be back tomorrow to check on him. True to my word, the next day after work I ran by his place to find him colorless and weak on the couch. There was not much discussion. I spoke, he listened, and we headed to the doctor's office.

At his initial appointment, they performed an EKG, ran blood work and some other tests. He woke the next morning actually feeling a little better, so he went to work as usual. I also got up, went to class then headed into work. The phone call came in to the museum around noon. The previous day's test results had come back, and he was directed to go to the hospital for a blood transfusion.

What? Blood transfusion? Why? He was clueless as to the reason, so I informed my boss that I would be leaving for the day, picked him up and drove to the hospital. He checked in once we arrived, and they whisked him to the back. Still in the dark as to what was actually going on, I was told that it would be a while until I could see him. I decided to run home, see our daughter and let my family know what was going on. A couple weeks before this we had found out that Mom had an aneurysm, so she was away on vacation in Vegas, relaxing and visiting my aunt before coming back for surgery.

Back at the hospital, the blood transfusion had helped return the color to his face, but there was still the question of what caused his loss of blood in the first place. Back at work again, another call came in, but this time the message on the other end was sadder than anything I had ever heard. It was cancer; they had administered a colonoscopy and found that the blood had been leaking from his colon on account of the cancer. Like a dark cloud that rolls in before a big storm is how it felt. I was terrified. On automatic pilot, I immediately went to the hospital, where they had already taken him into surgery to see the extent of the damage. An hour or so after I arrived, a doctor met me in the hallway and explained that on opening him up, even they were shocked to find that the cancer had already metastasized to his liver, lymph nodes and to his lungs. There was nothing they could do but close him back up.

"So what does that mean?" I asked.

"I'm sorry, but your ex-husband has terminal stage four cancer."

It felt as if someone had punched me in the stomach. The tears came instantly, and all I could do was lean against the wall behind me. The words were swimming around in my head: cancer... terminal. A million thoughts were running through my mind. "My best friend is going to die, colon cancer… He's only twenty-eight years old; the man that I loved for so many years is being taken away, the father of my child." Then it really hit me. "Oh my God, how do I tell my five-year-old baby that her daddy is going to die?"

Somehow I pulled myself together, slowly walked across the hall and opened the door to his room. There was no hiding what we were both feeling. We were too close and had known each other for too long to fake it. There wasn't a reason for either of us to say anything. Words weren't what was needed right then. I climbed in bed beside him. We just laid there and cried in each other's arms.

This was all like something out of a really bad dream. The next few weeks were long and stressful. I notified his mom and sister, who got on a bus from Kansas to come see him. By now, my mom had had her surgery, but at least that was healing nicely. The staff members at the hospital deli knew me by name since I practically lived there.

I'm not sure how I did it, but each morning, I woke up, got the baby ready for school, went to the hospital to check on him, went to class, then worked for a few hours, had lunch with him back at the hospital and then went back to work. Two nights a week, I also had evening classes; but I always went by the hospital to tell him goodnight. Then, I went home.

He was in the hospital for two weeks. We were able to talk about how we were going to deal with this situation, but the first thing I needed him to know was that he would not have to do this alone. Regardless of our marital status, we would always be family, so upon his release from the hospital, I brought him home. He needed time and space to heal, so the little one slept with me and I fixed her room up for him so he could be as comfortable as possible.

It got harder to watch him go through this because the chemotherapy made him so sick and weak. He would come home and try so hard to sleep, but the poison that they used to treat the disease caused major discomfort and constant vomiting, even when there was nothing in his stomach to expel. This went on for a couple months until he decided to stop treatment. He told me that he would rather enjoy the rest of his time left rather than always feeling weak and tired. This was his decision to make and my responsibility to accept, so I supported him. Over the next few months, he regained his strength and began to live life again.

He and I had talked about possibly making it work between us again, but this proved short-lived. In one weekend, that whole idea went straight out the window. You see, now that he felt good again, he decided to take a weekend trip up to Raleigh with his business partner. Good times hanging out and partying it up, like the old days. Well, when he came home on Sunday, I was in bed sick, and my mom had called The Rebound to come and take her to the store. As my ex-husband pulled into the driveway he saw The Rebound leaving the house with my mom and assumed he had been there to see me, which was not the case. Regardless, he stormed in the door, intending to chastise me. This was the first and last actual fight that my ex-husband and I would ever have. He screamed and yelled about how sorry I was for having another man at the house while he was gone, blah blah blah. In response, I just asked him to please keep his voice down because my head was killing me, which was why I had been in the bed all day.

Next thing I knew I was out of the bed screaming and yelling back at him, and then some terrible words came out of my mouth. "You can go to Hell!" Given the circumstances, that was a very hurtful thing to say, and it was too late to take it back, but his reaction to my words was of the utmost disrespect. His expression turned cold, and he spat in my face. Agh! I was mortified. I had to remove myself from the situation, and as I turned to walk away, he tried to kick me, but merely grazed my leg as I exited the door.

This was the worst of times for us. His condition got the best of us, and we both handled it very poorly. He moved out shortly after that incident, but not before we sat down and apologized to each other for allowing our emotions to get so out of control. Despite the alcoholism, the divorce and the minor disagreements; we were best friends. We could tell each other anything. This man whose name I still carry was a Great father, a kind soul who would give the shirt off of his back and the most honest man I have ever met.

It wasn't long before he settled into his new place and he had actually started dating again. This was a good thing because it gave him purpose and renewed the energy he had lost for a while. I was also ready for a new start, so I learned the ropes of the new, online dating scene. I managed to meet and talk with some really nice people until one day, a particular gentleman contacted me from Virginia.

At thirty years old, I was very intrigued by this man who was ten years my senior. Wow, could he ever talk! The Charmer was an excellent conversationalist as well as creative story writer. We started talking in April 2001, and within a couple of weeks I was hooked. The love letters that he would write me and the kindness of his words were so beautiful. There had to be a catch, right? Yep! He was married. I instantly put on the brakes. Little good it did me, though. He explained that he was not happy, and that he had not been so for many years, but had stayed for the sake of his son. I believed him.

Over the next couple months things got even more intense, to the degree of us using the words "I Love You", even though we had never met in person. We finally made arrangements for him to visit me in North Carolina. We were both excited, and counting down the days until we would meet.

June came and so did the knock on my door. Our first hug and kiss were absolutely breathtaking. We spent the entire weekend wrapped up in each other, eating, sleeping and making love. Yes, I slept with him upon meeting him the first time. My life – my decision. When the time came for us to say goodbye we had already made plans to see each other again.

Since he drove all the way to me the first time, our next visit would be the following month, half way between his house and mine. The timing for this just so happened to fall on his birthday. If you think I was already in over my head, wait until you find out what I gave him for his gift.

July quickly approached and it was time for our next rendezvous. After a nice walk and a good meal, we went back to the hotel where I, surprisingly, read something that I wrote to him. Then, looking directly into his eyes, I took his hand, slipped a ring on his finger and asked him to marry me. Without hesitation and with tears in his eyes, he answered "Yes!"

Now, we both know that this situation was far from ideal, but I was so happy. I recall driving to Virginia one Saturday afternoon, just to see him for a few hours before I had to get back on the road and head home. Then came 9/11, and knowing that he worked in close proximity to the Pentagon, I was a nervous wreck until he called me and I heard his voice. We already had plans for the following weekend and felt that, because of recent events, seeing each other meant even more than before.

Our next meeting took place at Pumpkin Hill, a beautiful chalet that sat atop a hill in the mountains of Virginia. It was so quiet and serene up there. There was no TV or city noise, only the two of us and the evening stars. The weekend was perfect, but like all the others, we had to part ways come Sunday morning.

The constant goodbyes made us want a permanent change. We both had preparations to make, but our plan was for me to get to Virginia full-time. While I spoke with my family and my ex about the move, The Charmer filed for legal separation and spoke with his father about our plans. Now this is where it really gets interesting.

December was D-Day; all of our things were packed up and ready to load onto the truck. I didn't just have his help and that of my family to move. His father, who was in his seventies, drove down from Pennsylvania, picked up The Charmer from Virginia, then headed for North Carolina to help us. Sorry, but this gesture spoke volumes to me about how our relationship would be perceived by his family. Upon arrival, his father gave me the biggest hug and thanked me for making his son so happy.

With everything loaded up, my daughter rode shotgun with his dad while The Charmer and I led the way with our rental truck, towing my car behind. We were Virginia-bound and ready to start our life together. It was about a five-hour drive before we pulled up at the house he had rented for us.

The place was empty but warm. We settled in for the night with plans to do all the unpacking the following day, still with the help of his dad. By Sunday evening, most things had been set up and put in their place. It did feel a little strange at first, being in a new town where I knew nobody, nor was there any family around. But I looked on it as a fresh start; as long as we were together, it would be okay. Well, that soon changed, for a couple of reasons.

Within a month of moving there, I was in constant communication with my ex-husband, who was declining rapidly. By this time, he had moved back to Kansas to be close to his family. They had already called a hospice, but final arrangements still needed to be made. I told The Charmer of my intention to visit my ex-husband in Kansas. I sensed that he didn't have much longer, and I wanted my daughter to see her father at least one more time. I asked my mother to come along with me, so I had help with the drive.

One morning I took off for North Carolina to pick up Mom. She, my baby and I headed west for Kansas. That was the worst trip I have ever had to make. We hadn't even made it out of North Carolina before the little one sat up in the back seat and threw up everywhere; front seat, back seat, everywhere. After pulling over on the side of a mountain to clean up a bit, we decided we would stop and get a room for the night, right across the Tennessee border.

The next day we got back on the road and resumed our journey. We finally reached our destination sometime around eleven that evening. The little one was wide awake and so very happy to see her daddy. We went in to sit and talk for a bit before going to my aunt's house, where my mom and I planned to stay.

I had known for a long time that he was going to die. I had been given the news first-hand, and we'd talked about it for over a year now, yet it still did not hit me that this was actually real until he came out of his room weighing maybe one hundred twenty pounds, hooked to an oxygen tank. Upon closing his door, we all saw the medical sign that read "DNR – Do Not Resuscitate." Once again I felt the wind had been knocked out of me.

It was so real now, but I had to stay strong. I was expected to be the one to keep it all together. He needed me to stay focused and to help him make the final preparations with which his family could not help. This included meeting with the funeral home to discuss his final wishes. He said that he did not want a funeral and that he wanted to be cremated. I was able to talk him into lying in wake for a while so that his friends and family would be able to pay their last respects. He wavered a bit, but then agreed. I told the funeral rep that I would be the one paying for all expenses and provided all my contact information.

Once the meeting was over, he asked one more thing of me.

"Anything," I told him.

"Please do not let our daughter see me lying in a casket. I want her to remember me the way I am now." I took a deep breath, than nodded.

We stayed there for a week, and leaving him was so hard. I was so torn between going back to the new life I had started, and being with my best friend until the very end. I didn't know what to do. I talked with my mother about it for a bit and decided that it would be best to go back. As strong as I was or thought I was, I truly didn't think I could have handled – the end. Before leaving, he asked me to lie beside him one more time, and I did. He was like a little boy in my arms and his now irregular heartbeat settled as he drifted off to sleep. This would be the last time we saw him.

Once I was back in Virginia, my ex-husband and I spoke a few more times over the next three weeks, but his pain and low energy level meant that these were very short conversations. The last time that I heard his voice was on Valentine's Day.

A couple of days later, The Charmer, my daughter and I were sitting in the living room watching TV. It was Presidents' Day so there was no work or school. In the middle of watching a movie, I stood up and went upstairs to use the bathroom. Funny thing was, we had a bathroom downstairs right across from the living room. The tingle in my tummy subsided as quickly as I got upstairs. I thought it odd, but something was off. I went back downstairs.

Within seconds of my sitting back down, the phone rang. I walked into the kitchen to answer it. "Hello?"

It was his sister – he was gone. No more pain, no more suffering. It was over. As I stood in the kitchen trying to take it all in, The Charmer noticed the look on my face and knew instantly what the call was about. He quickly came and put his arms around me as I slowly melted into nothing. I had no idea what that type of pain felt like. Never before in my life had I experienced something that made me feel so helpless, sad, scared and completely out of sync.

Even worse, I still had to walk across the hall and tell my daughter that her daddy had died. I walked over and picked her up, sat her on my lap and uttered those dreadful words. Her little face went blank and tears fell from her eyes. On February 18, 2002, my daughter lost her father, and I lost my best friend. It was a very, very sad day.

CHAPTER 3 Part 2
The Lost Years

The tension that had been mounting between The Charmer and his wife boiled over on the very next day. Threats and guilt took hold, and as we sat on the couch that evening he broke the news that he needed to go back to the other house "for now". I was surprised that this did not upset me. All I could think about was getting through the loss of my ex and taking care of my daughter. I actually felt that it would be best for me to mourn his loss without The Charmer. I did not come out and tell him that, but my acceptance of my fiancé's moving back in with his ex was a clear sign that it was the best thing for us at that time.

Much of the next few months were a blur. The Charmer was still a regular fixture around the house but I tried to remain focused on the little one, pouring everything I had into her. I never fully understood the concept of grief, even with me in my third year of college as a psychology major. All I could do was wonder when the pain and crying would stop, and try with all my being to avoid transferring this misery onto my daughter.

She was only six at the time, so I think that helped make things easier for her until, one night after I had put her to bed, she called me back into her room. I sat on the edge of her bed and asked her what was wrong. She instantly started to cry. I figured she was just nervous because she was going to be performing in her school play the following day.

"Baby, what's the matter?" I asked again. She quietly explained to me that "This will be the first time that my daddy will not be there to watch me."

My heart sank to the pit of my stomach. I comforted her best I could without breaking down, but once I returned to my room where The Charmer was waiting, I couldn't hold myself together any longer. All I wanted to do was curl up into a little ball, and that's exactly what I did.

Things slowly started getting back to normal as spring was winding down. We had a pleasant treat bestowed upon us by The Charmer's dad. The Charmer had seven siblings, so when they could get together, it was pretty special. With my little one and me becoming new additions to the clan, his father sent out the word that there would be a festive gathering at his place in Pennsylvania to welcome us to the family.

Everyone was in attendance that weekend except his younger sister, who was unable to make it in from Montana. His other three sisters were there. Two lived in Pennsylvania, and the other flew in from Wyoming. All three of his brothers, who resided in Pennsylvania, were there too. We received a very warm welcome from everyone, though with the divorce talk floating in the air, it was still a little awkward. The overall consensus was that The Charmer had finally found someone he loved and who loved him back. I couldn't have asked for a better group of people to call family. That was only the first of many wonderful trips that we took to Pennsylvania.

That fall, I finally got back on track with school and transferred my studies from Fayetteville State University of North Carolina to George Mason University in Virginia. It turned out I would have to attend an additional year for residency requirements, but I didn't mind. I just wanted to finish what I had started. Also, we were beginning to look and act like a real family. The little one had just finished her first season on the summer swim team. The Charmer's son was spending time at our house on a more regular basis, and all the financial requirements for child and spousal support had been set by the courts.

As we toyed with a date for our marriage, I began working on my gown. I found the perfect pattern by Vera Wang in a *Vogue* book. Although I had dabbled at sewing for some time, I had never taken on a project like this. It was so exciting, and every free moment I had was spent toiling away on the gown.

At the same time, we began talking about having a baby. This was a touchy little subject with me because three years after I had my daughter I had gone in for a tubal ligation. I thought I was done, but there was something about the thought of having a baby with him that made me giddy. I had watched him over the past year and a half with his son and my daughter, and knew beyond the shadow of a doubt that he would be a great father to our child.

After a little internet research, some phone calls and serious discussions, I was slotted for surgery down in Chapel Hill, North Carolina to have a tubal reversal.

It was to be a short weekend trip, down and back with no complications.

Success – all went well. Though painful and disheartening to have a long scar on my tummy, it was well worth it. We were instructed to wait three months before trying to conceive, which we did, and by the middle of the fourth month I was pregnant. We were excited and thrilled that it happened so quickly. Just like the typical woman, I began picking up little things here and there. While in North Carolina for the procedure, we sat up one night thinking of names. Without any conflict whatsoever, we chose two. If it were a boy, his name would be Tristan Johan, but if a little girl were to grace our lives, her name was to be Siana Skye.

Summer was here again, and we were in the thick of the swimming season. There was practice four nights a week, Friday morning fun time and 7 am

Saturday meets for eight weeks. That meant 5 am rise and shine each and every Saturday morning. I actually enjoyed it more than my daughter did some days.

At one of these, a home meet at the park, we arrived as always with gear in hand. Parent participation is a big part of this sport, and I was used to running around cheering, timing and helping out where I could. But on this particular day I was sitting down in the back with my feet up taking it easy. I felt a little funny this time but figured it was just gas. Pregnancy will do that to a woman.

The Charmer took my place helping out the kids and his dad, who had come down to watch the little one swim, kept an eye on me, as did many of my friends whose kids were also on the team. I thought it would ease up after a while sitting still, but it never did. It just got more and more uncomfortable as I sat there. Stubborn by nature, I refused to leave the meet early.

No matter what, I was going to be there to watch my baby swim. Once the meet was over, we went home; I took some medicine, lay down and quickly fell asleep.

The next morning, I felt fine. I didn't understand what had happened the day before, but I was glad the pain was gone. I went into the kitchen and began cooking breakfast, but suddenly this sharp pain shot through my stomach. I was barely able to make it over to the couch, and to be touched or moved was excruciating.

The Charmer wanted to carry me to the car, but I begged him not to touch me. The only other option was to call an ambulance, and that's what he did. Within minutes, they were wheeling me out and loading me into the vehicle. The pain terrified me.

We got to the hospital, where the medics rushed into action to find the cause of the pain. After an extremely painful internal sonogram (another reason men should be thankful that they're men), they discovered the problem. The pregnancy was not in my uterus as it should have been. It was actually in my left fallopian tube, and the natural progression of fetus growth had ruptured the tube. I was bleeding internally, which is very painful and, I learnt, can lead to death.

With nothing more to be said, they carted me off to the operating room for emergency surgery to stop the bleeding and remove the damaged tube. It was a sad thing that we lost the baby, but we didn't get discouraged because we knew we would try again. The medical staff advised us to give my body time to heal before trying again. This was actually a good time to do just that, because I was on course to finish up school within the next few months. So we took a break from the baby-making for a bit.

I bought my first home in August 2003. It felt so good that, at the age of 33, I had finally become a homeowner. Most of my pride in this purchase derived from the fact that I had financed it on my own. Although The Charmer was there and contributed to the household expenses, there was only so much left over after he paid for the upkeep and support of his family across town. Besides, there was no way that I was going to take the risk of combining our names on the mortgage while there was a possibility of his wife laying claim to it.

This little abode that I purchased was a frightful sight initially; even my realtor looked at me sideways when I told her I wanted to make an offer. But, being the fixer-upper I am, I rolled up my sleeves and we got right down to business.

The house was built in 1965 and sat on a two-acre corner lot. It had not been maintained for a while. The basement was wet and dated; the dark brown wood paneling that adorned the walls was far from appropriate. It needed paint throughout, flooring, new windows, and both bathrooms and the kitchen required complete remodeling.

Talk about having a good time. My girlfriend was going through major turmoil in her marriage, so being the supportive and caring friend that I am, I invited her over for a day of sledgehammer therapy. Within a matter of hours, the upstairs bathroom was gutted. Home improvement stores became our home away from home. We spent hours upon hours traveling back and forth for paint, lighting, doors, tools, flooring and so much more. Before we knew it, the house felt like a home.

January 2004 came, and it was time for me to walk across the stage. My family proudly watched the commencement ceremony that awarded me my Bachelor of Arts degree in Psychology. The most important part of that day was to have my daughter witness that it is never too late to get your education. Never mind that it would not be an option for her – it was more of a family requirement!

What to do with my degree then became the big question. To work productively in my chosen field, I would have to continue on in graduate school. While tossing around a few ideas and options, I began substitute teaching at a local high school.

When school ended for the year, we found out that I was pregnant again. This time I knew that before doing anything else I had to go directly to the hospital for them to check the placement of the embryo.

Unfortunately, The Charmer was in Bethesda with his ex at the time because she had collapsed a couple days earlier at church from an aneurism, so my girlfriend went with me. I was pretty confident that everything would be okay, but the prognosis was the same as before. I wigged out a little more this time, telling the doctor that he was a liar and to leave me alone. But I soon came back to reality and signed the papers so they could surgically flush my one remaining tube. One small consolation was that this time they were able to salvage the tube so we could try again in the future.

During the follow up-exam with my regular gynecologist, she looked at me straight and said, "Sweetie, your poor little body can't take much more of this." This was my fourth surgery in five years. I agreed. Our next option was to venture into the world of in vitro fertilization, and that's when things began to get expensive. We were no closer to getting married, yet this baby thing had taken center stage. We were optimistic about the process, and went at it guns blazing. Of course, the funny part was the standard male collection. Since most of the process involves the woman, I felt it only fitting to chuckle as he made that lone journey into the solitary play room.

With everything that needed to be done, this venture was remarkably time-consuming. The weekly office visits, the prescription pick-ups and the shots began to take their toll, but before we completely lost our minds, it was time to go in for the insemination. Not a difficult feat at all, it took less than an hour. The hard part was going home and waiting for the results.

I remember it being a nice cool day, so all the blinds and windows were open throughout the house. Coming down the hallway from the bedroom, I heard the phone ring. The news was not good. As I thanked the caller and hung up the phone, The Charmer and I looked at each other with defeat all over our faces. After two years and thirty thousand dollars, we had to throw in the towel. Let's face it, this was just not meant to be.

I still believe that on that day, our relationship began its descent. To be honest, it was all going backwards anyway. What made us think we would be blessed with a happily ever after, when there were so many obstacles that we were jumping over, instead of clearing them properly from our path? From the combination of his family asking what was taking him so long with the divorce, people asking me when we were going to get married, being unable to have a baby, and the rest of life's everyday trials, it broke.

I had already stopped asking about his divorce paperwork the year prior. The pressure increased when a fight that had started at the house across town came into my home. The Charmer and his son walked in and headed straight for the back bedroom. I could hear raised voices and words that should not have been spoken around my daughter. Never having been in that type of environment, she ran out of her room and asked me, "What is going on in there?" She had this scared, puppy-dog look on her face that was almost funny – but not really. Because of my upbringing, this was nothing new to me, but it was not something I wanted her ever to be around.

"Baby, go back to your room and put your headphones on," I told her. "I'll check on you in a little bit."

With her safely tucked away in her room, Momma had to go to work. I threw open that bedroom door and barked, "Where in the Hell do you think you are? You two must have forgotten that you're not at 1234 Shoot-em-Up Drive. This type of behavior is not allowed in MY HOUSE!" They both froze.

I told The Charmer to go to the living room. Then, after speaking with his son for a bit, I advised him to step outside and take a walk.

The very next month, driving back from North Carolina, I told The Charmer that I wanted him to move out. That's when he finally revealed what all the tension and fussing had been about. I thought it was just everyday growing pains that he and his son were going through, but I was way off. The real reason was that a couple months before all of this, his wife had been diagnosed with breast cancer. The Charmer thought that keeping such important information from me would prevent worry. It didn't matter to me what his reasoning was because by that point, I was done, and I told him to go home.

I didn't let any grass grow under my feet either. One of my destructive flaws is that I have usually vacated a relationship emotionally long before I actually leave. Within the week, I had plans to meet The Rocker. Okay, he wasn't in a band or anything, but he definitely looked the part; completely the opposite of the last one. Instead of being ten years older, this one was ten years younger than me. He was a free-spirited, hardworking party guy. I didn't have to tip-toe around any issues. I could do what I wanted without judgment or inquisition. He was thrilled to be with an older woman that he perceived as having her stuff together, and I enjoyed his sexy youthfulness.

Now, even though he didn't have two nickels to rub together, I moved full-speed ahead. He was sharing a room with his "best-friend" at her mother's house when I met him. This didn't really faze me, though, because I was not trying to start anything serious. We just hung out, took some road trips and had fun.

A snag hit when his car clunked out on him. Either I would have to make the trip to see him every time, or I could help him out with the car situation. Over the next few weeks, we searched for a new vehicle for him. He knew what he wanted and just had to find one that was worth buying. Finally, we found the car he liked, and I went to the bank, drew $4,500 from my savings account and bought him a car. No, I didn't have money like that, trust me. He paid me back a little each month over the next year.

Five months in, the attachment grew a little stronger, and I gave him the ultimatum to move in with me or stay there with her, but stop seeing me. As long as there was no official title for us, The Rocker sharing a room with another female was of no concern to me, but it was evident that we were more than friends. I could not have him sleeping with her, and yes, there was more going on than just covering up, closing eyes and beginning to snore. Needless to say, he chose the former option and moved in.

Things were pretty hunky dory with The Rocker and me, even though he was still tipping across town a bit, until the anniversary of my break-up with The

Charmer came around. When it ended, I had asked The Charmer for a year to figure things out and take some time for myself. Well, I wasn't by myself, and I hadn't figured out anything in regard to him and me. I was unsure of us meeting at this point but, just like so many other crazy choices I had made in the past, I moved backward, full-speed – in reverse.

The Charmer and I arranged a meeting place and time to talk about our future. We were cordial at first, but as these talks progressed, resentment, anger and blame surfaced. He blamed me for the breakdown of our relationship, claiming that if I had really loved him I would have waited forever for him. He also claimed that he had loved and treated me better than most husbands who were bound by that sheet of paper.

I told him that wasn't good enough. I wanted and deserved more. I was also worthy of having my own husband rather than someone else's. I went home and told The Rocker some of what had transpired between me and The Charmer. He asked me what I was going to do, and I said I didn't know.

This next part is what I fear may tarnish my daughter forever. For the next two and a half years, I flip-flopped back and forth between these two men. It would be six months with The Charmer, then six months with The Rocker. My life was spiraling out of control.

Already stretched on funds, I decided to follow through with plans to remodel my home. The cost was $125,000. Blood, sweat and tears got it done. Now, with a $2,500 monthly mortgage, my current job as a school photographer wasn't quite cutting it. In January 2008, I began applying for jobs with the government, not just for the income, but for the stability. I still had both men around, but I was my sole source of support.

Bills were piling up, and my stress level was through the roof.

There was good and bad news on the horizon. Good news first: I got offered a job with the Department of the Army. Hoorah! Bad news time: my new job came just a little too late to catch up on what had fallen so far behind. I swallowed my pride, clenched my teeth and filed for bankruptcy. I told myself this was rock-bottom – or so I thought.

Two months later, I'm with The Rocker again, and guess what? I'm pregnant. Really? This was happening now? I had just gotten comfortable in my new job and was trying to get back on my feet.

I followed protocol like before. I went to the hospital for the internal sonogram. This time it was too early to tell where the baby had taken up residence. The next day, when I came home from work, the full-on pain was back. I told my daughter to get her things so I could drop her off at our friend's house; she knew the drill by now. I went upstairs to tell The Rocker that we needed to leave immediately. He was not at all pleased because he was "tired". So when he asked if he could wear his pajama bottoms, I told him I would just drive myself. He recognized my frustration and took me after all, but he did keep those ridiculous pants on.

We arrived at the hospital around seven that evening. By eleven, the pain and his tired attitude made me want to scream. I finally got back the test confirming what I already knew. The Rocker sat in a chair beside the bed, and the doctor asked whether I wanted them to flush or remove the tube.

Sarcastically, but with all seriousness at the same time, I said, "Alex, I'll take 'Removal of the Tube' for 100, please." I never wanted to go through this again. I removed all my jewelry, handed it to the Rocker and told him to go home. I would be fine on my own, and I waited for them to put me to sleep for the fifth time.

I opened my eyes, and like always, I looked around to reorient myself with my surroundings. I thanked God for waking me up. Then without fail, the pain reminded me of why I was actually there. This time to my surprise, they had been able to do the surgery through laparoscopy, which meant I could go home as soon as my ride got there. Unfortunately for me, they couldn't get a hold of The Rocker by cell or house phone because he was sleeping, so I called my girlfriend to come get me from the hospital. When I got home and saw him sound asleep, I could have set the bed on fire with him in it. That was my final stint with The Rocker, but we parted as friends.

Along with the financial chaos came the mortgage hounds, who chose to foreclose rather than work with me. In five years with this company, I had never been late or missed a payment. When I called to notify them that I would be two months late with payment because of medical issues, they started the paperwork. How amazing that they were one of the first companies to ask for help with the bail-out, but brushed off loyal clients who had also fallen on hard times. Anyway, they wanted to take the house before Christmas, but the judge told them no. I could have waited around for the official kick-out, but instead we packed up and moved into a rental not far from the old house.

Now get this: after my bankruptcy was discharged in February and we were settling into the new place, these idiots had the audacity to call me for a possible loan modification on the house! Seriously, I wanted to laugh, but it really wasn't funny. I was insulted. I politely told the representative that I was no longer interested in working with her company and that the property was currently empty for them to do with as they pleased.

You could have bought this lady for a penny. She began asking me questions like, "Is the house being maintained? Does it still have power and water?"

I asked her, "Why would I maintain a house with power and water if I no longer live there?"

She quickly informed me that they would need to hasten the possession, then. I told her, "That's fine with me. I did lock it up."

In the midst of this madness, I decided to enter therapy. I felt like I needed an unbiased party to help me put all that had transpired over the past few years into perspective. I could not allow it to fester into something unproductive. I was, and always will be, well aware that God is the healer of all things. But I also needed that personal, one-on-one human interaction with tangible feedback. Therapy turned out well. There were still some things that needed work in my personal life but, by the end of February 2009, I had "cleaned house". There was no more back-and-forth relationship between The Charmer and The Rocker, my job was going well, and the new house felt like home.

For the next couple months, it was so easy to breathe. I was happy. If I wanted to go out with friends, I could. If I wanted to go on a date I would. The not-so-little one and I were doing great. It actually felt good to know that I was capable of stepping out of my comfort zone and meeting new people.

I made a list and worked on what I really wanted and needed in a partner. I didn't want to rush or settle for just anyone, so I started keeping my eyes open for "Red Flags". You know, those things that should make a person run the other way. When I met someone and a flag went up, I would break contact. There was no point in wasting my time or theirs. Just in case you've lost track, I was now a mere thirty-eight years young.

Well, in watching out for these flags, I still made use of my online resources. One day I made plans to meet The Bachelor. He was a blue-eyed twenty-eight-year-old cutie. He had a good job, no kids, owned a home and was super-sweet. Right off the bat we got along really well. We talked and laughed about everything. He also had a cool motorcycle on which I could ride with him. That in itself was big, because in this area I was not getting on the back of a bike with just anyone. There were rules to be followed, and he made sure I was compliant: helmet –check; gloves – check; pants – check; jacket – check. I felt completely safe, and all I had to do was hold on.

As time went along, I noticed something about The Bachelor that gave me pause. It wasn't a bad thing, just a noteworthy observance. His "me" time and his toys were very precious to him. Also, when we spoke of marriage and kids, he was absent. What I mean by this is that he was indifferent, still in the "I don't know" stage of his life.

I knew that one day I wanted to remarry, but wasn't going to shove it down anyone's throat. On the child side of the house, it was not negotiable. I could not have, nor did I want, any more children. So only two months in, the marriage issue was a moot point. Just the thought of him wanting a child of his own one day stopped things cold. He explained that he didn't think he wanted any, but he just wasn't sure.

"I will not be the one that holds up the possibility of you having a family someday. Even though you don't think you will want that right now, you could in the future, and then where does that leave us? I don't want there to be bitterness and resentment if it were to come to that. Being a parent has been the greatest joy of my life, and I wouldn't dare be the person that could prevent you from experiencing that for yourself."

And that was that.

He wasn't happy with my response, and wanted us to work. I remember driving home from his house in tears one night because, as bad as I wanted it to work too, I couldn't do it.

It just so happened that within the same week, The Bachelor was going on a planned, three-week jaunt around the country on his bike, and my daughter and I were headed out to California for summer vacation. This made it easier for me to move on since we would be apart for a while. I think we might have talked once during his trip, but it was okay because along came a soldier from across the water.

Scanning through profiles on my computer, I came across one that told a story the likes of which were rare in this particular forum. I couldn't help but notice that we had many commonalities. He was in the service, I had once served. He had a teenage son, I a teenage daughter. We were both divorced, and we both had a mutual love of music.

The Embellisher and I began corresponding over the next couple of months, getting to know one another. Our conversations were pleasant and light on account of his current deployment status. Also, when he was stateside, he resided four hours from me in North Carolina. I actually had family in the same town, so there was a chance that it could work.

As October approached, we were both about to celebrate our birthdays, which were only seven days apart. He would be turning thirty-three and me, thirty-nine. Our correspondence had become daily. Then we evolved to video chatting so we could see each other.

We talked every day when he woke up in the morning and I was settling in for the night.

With things still in their infancy, it was me that broke the ice about a relationship. He received the revelation of my crush well enough, but not without pause. I learnt that The Embellisher had scars from his last trip across the water. He had received a Dear John letter from his fiancée, informing him that all of his things would be waiting for him in a storage unit when he got home.

Now, I could see how that would make anyone a little gun shy about starting something new while being so far away, but I reassured him that I had no intention of hurting him and that I would wait for him to get back.

Our chatting sessions turned a little more sappy, with cute little smiley faces, automated kisses and the touching "I Miss You". We were also able to talk on the phone during the day because of where I worked, so the lines of communication were wide open for us. The only problem was that some of the important things we should have discussed, we avoided. Little by little, he revealed some things about his life, like having his son while still in high school, and not graduating from there until he was twenty years old. I blame myself for not asking the hard questions, but I just figured I would have a chance to get all the details once he returned to the States.

Since I am who I am, the cards, letters and gifts began to take flight. The holidays were upon us, and I wanted him to share in my joy, even though he was oceans away. My daughter and I spent quality time in the kitchen baking homemade cookies for him. She was busy manning the peanut butter bars while I diligently took charge of mastering the delicious oatmeal raisin cookies. Those were his favorite. Along with these special goodies, I prepared a package that contained a Christmas tree with lights and a variety of standard ornaments, along with a few that were personalized. He thanked me for the many gifts that we sent, and in return sent me some items he thought I would like. With technology on our side, on Christmas morning I was able to watch him open the gifts I had sent.

Aware that the New Year would soon follow, I had already prepared something to make it special for the both of us. He received a box a few days after Christmas that he was not allowed to open until New Year's Eve. We discussed plans for me to get off work early on New Year's Eve so that I would be home in time for the clock to strike midnight, his time.

Like every day before, I got to work that morning and made my daily phone call to him. All was set for that evening. We would have the opportunity to bring in the New Year together–only it never happened.

Two days later, The Embellisher resurfaced as though nothing was wrong. I couldn't believe it! When I asked him what happened, he simply stated, "Sorry. I couldn't wake up." I was so completely dumbfounded; I actually just let it drop. Though I wondered what had happened to the personalized, $75 bottle of sparkling apple cider I had sent to him for our official toast.

Although we were still talking, the relationship began to taper off as his return home came closer. Another good friend, a soldier himself, warned me about the effects of deployment and the behavior that often follows on returning. He advised me to give The Embellisher time and space to decompress. So as he readied to leave, I stepped back and waited for him to reach out to me. Adding to his frustration, his return date was pushed back twice, so what was supposed to be six months turned into eight.

Word came, and he was on his way. Flying here, then there, he finally returned to American soil. I knew there would be a lot to do once he got back, so I didn't expect to hear from him right away. To my surprise, he called me at the office the day after he came home. I had been in a training class, but during my lunch break I checked in with my office, and they told me I'd missed his call. I also had a missed call on my cell phone, so I quickly called him to welcome him home.

Two weeks later I'd heard nothing more, and my patience was growing a little thin. Either way, I wanted to know what this was or what it wasn't. It was a Wednesday afternoon when we talked, and I told him I was heading to North Carolina for the weekend if he wanted to meet in person.

His answer was, "If you are coming this way, sure." This was evidence that he'd been telling the truth when he said he was more logical than romantic. We made plans to meet at a Mexican restaurant we both knew. Having lived in the same town for more than nine years, I knew the place quite well.

I wasn't as nervous as I was anxious. I just wanted it to be over. Walking along the sidewalk near our meeting place, I watched as he pulled in. He walked right over to where I was. We hugged, and then headed inside to grab a bite to eat. We sat and talked for a couple hours before leaving so that he could run to Raleigh to pick up a television stand and stereo equipment that he had ordered.

Standing outside the restaurant by my truck we hugged and had our first kiss. This continued for about twenty minutes or so, but I finally told him that he would be late if he didn't leave then. He promised to call on his way back, and then he left.

That night as I was lying upstairs watching television, my phone rang. It was The Embellisher letting me know that he was on his way back to town. He asked if he could see me and we decided that since he was already out, he would just come to where I was staying. We cuddled up with each other on the couch and went to sleep.

The next morning, I woke him up to leave. He was planning to get his place in order after being gone for so long. There was a television delivery scheduled, and he needed to get everything synced and organized. By five, I still hadn't heard from him, so I called and asked what he was doing. He was just sitting at home, watching movies on his computer. So, obviously my response to him was, "Aren't we supposed to be spending the day together?" His reply, "Then why aren't you over here?" I never imagined he would be this much work!

During many of our conversations, The Embellisher mentioned living in a small place because he was unable to afford much more, based on his income. I knew his rank, and I knew that he had a child, so it seemed a little odd, but I didn't think much of it. As I pulled up to his place I realized that "small" was an understatement. A person could go stir crazy in a place that size, but at least it was warm and provided a roof over his head I guess. Besides, I didn't care about that sort of thing. I just wanted to spend time with him. I won't go into detail, but I will say that I spent my entire night with him and by morning, our relationship was on to the next level.

We awoke, showered and got ourselves ready to go have breakfast. As we sat eating and chit-chatting away, The Embellisher's face suddenly went solemn. He remained quiet for a moment, then started in with, "There are some things I feel you should know – things that I didn't want to talk about while I was away." He expressed that he was not proud of what he was about to tell me. Then it came out. "I don't only have one child. I actually have three."

Wow, that was pretty big, but it finally made sense why his money was so tight. Having three children was expensive. I think he was somewhat surprised that I didn't automatically head for the door when he shared this information. On the contrary, I told him that it was okay. After breakfast, he drove us back to his place so that I could pick up my truck. It was time to head back to Virginia. What came next stung me to my core. As we were saying our goodbyes, I bluntly asked him what we were going to do next. He proceeded to tell me he wasn't sure and that we would talk about it later. No, I wanted to talk about it right then and there! After everything that had happened and everything I was doing for this "relationship', I deserved to know what was going on.

He babbled on about not being ready and being unable to give me what I needed due to his situation, yadda yadda. I was tired and worn from it all. I didn't even know what to say anymore. What I should have been doing was counting all the Red Flags that were flying. I started to cry and then simply drove away.

I've come to realize one of my biggest problems: the way I picture things turning out in my head is not usually how they pan out. As the phenomenal Maya Angelou would say, "When someone shows you who they are, believe them." Honestly, I don't believe in fairy tales because, if you actually take the time to study these fables, they consist of broken families. Stepmothers, sisters and fathers, witchery, greed and lies – those are the things of which childhood stories are made.

Back home, still reeling from what had just transpired over the previous forty-eight hours, I was a complete mess. My best bet would have been to call off work the next day, but I've always been a little stingy with my leave, so I bit the bullet and went in, swollen eyes and all. My boys at work knew the purpose of my trip and were curious as to how it went. All I could do was shake my head with an obvious expression of not wanting to talk about it. By the end of the day, I had told a few of them what happened during my weekend with The Embellisher.

By the end of that week, I was feeling better, and reached out via email. I told him that he didn't owe me anything, and although my feelings were hurt I did not regret meeting him. That gesture on my part prompted a telephone call from him the next day. This time, he opened up a little more about his kids and how he had actually been married twice, not just once, and that the three children were by three different women. I wondered why he hadn't disclosed all of this information on his profile, and why he didn't tell me all of this before. His excuse was that he was ashamed of his past. He thought that if he shared this up front, nobody would want to date him.

I told him that none of us was perfect, but for him to be so misleading was wrong. He apologized. I accepted. After that, he randomly asked me if I would like to attend his unit's Spring Formal. I'm sure by now you can guess my answer. Wow, Grandma, what charisma you have!

Over the next couple months, things were pretty good. He made it a point to take me to his favorite restaurant. Then back at the house we took our first official picture together, and he kept it in the gauge window of his truck. We took turns on the visits. One weekend I was down there, the next weekend he came to Virginia. We burned through a lot of gas and tire tread.

At the time, he was big into his archery hobby, so we planned to travel to Florida in July. Things felt more and more comfortable, and a couple weeks before our upcoming trip, I was down there with him for my scheduled weekend visit, when I said it: I told The Embellisher that I loved him. He didn't have a response to my words, but I wasn't expecting him to. I felt the need to say it.

I went home to Virginia, only to turn right back around the following weekend for our trip. It wasn't too bad, though, because he drove the whole eight hours down to Florida. Once there, we scoped out the Archery Club before heading to our hotel to check in.

We did a little shopping, ate some good meals, and he was able to participate in his first Florida shoot in years. It turned out to be a really good time. Since we had taken leave to make it a four-day weekend, we headed back to North Carolina Sunday afternoon so that we could still have one day to chill and relax. We got back to town at a decent time, so we grabbed some food and went to the house to rest. That evening as we were lying on the couch watching TV, very sweetly, The Embellisher whispered in my ear, "I love you." I told him that I loved him too, and he said he had wanted to tell me that all weekend.

Even though it appeared to be going well for us, there were still some things that struck me as odd about him – like the fact that he didn't have any friends. His personality and social skills were not accepted by most. He had been removed from his position at work because there were constant conflicts with other soldiers. An equal employment opportunity complaint had been filed against him, though it was ultimately dismissed. When he came to visit me, there was no dialogue between him and my daughter. If she tried to speak to him, it seemed to make him uncomfortable. He was good with our dog, though.

I've always tried to focus on the good things that I see in people. He had given me some sweet gifts, and always had the drinks and snacks I liked on hand when I came into town. Also, he was very good at reaching out to me. His topic of choice might have been mainly what was going on in his world, but he diligently called and texted me throughout every day. I was well aware of the good and bad within this relationship.

The next major event coming up was my "Fabulous and Forty Birthday Party". I was so excited; it was going to be awesome! I really looked forward to turning forty years old. Most cringed at the idea, but not me. By the first of September, invitations were sent out and there would be twenty-five to thirty people in attendance from Virginia, North Carolina and Texas.

My family and The Embellisher were scheduled to arrive on Friday, my actual birthday, but the party would take place the next evening. That Saturday, everyone scurried to get things in order for the event. My sister and I had errands to run for some last-minute supplies, while The Embellisher – I think to avoid awkward dealings with my family – decided to head to the archery range.

As the event drew closer, I was still running around getting things together until The Embellisher shuttled me upstairs to get dressed. This is where he presented me with my birthday gift. He smiled at the fact that this was also reflected on my Birthday Cake – a string of pearls. I didn't wear them that evening though because I had chosen to wear the beautiful pendant he got me the month before.

We headed downstairs, and the party got under way. The night was great; good food, good music and lots of friends and family. I spent most of my night outside dancing, and he sort of wandered around inside. My sister was completely annoyed with his unwillingness to dance with me at least once, but I refused to let it dampen my spirit. It was MY day. Overall, the event was a success, and I had a total blast.

The next weekend, we celebrated the birthdays of my daughter and The Embellisher. I planned a trip down to North Carolina Thursday night as a surprise for his birthday. I would be back on Sunday to be with my daughter for hers on Monday.

My trip down was pleasant, and he was excited to see me with gifts in hand. We went out to grab something to eat and then back to the house for the evening. I gave him one final surprise. There was a knock on the door and a special delivery – a dozen red roses for him and him alone.

We began to do the research and planning for our next trip together, which was supposed to be for a week in February of the upcoming year. That's when the annual archery competition would be held in Vegas. Due to his financial obligations and my belief in partnership, I told him I would pay half of the cost, so we sat down one afternoon at my house and booked our travel. He paid for his airfare and the hotel, and I paid for my airfare and the rental car.

Our next visit was not a good one. He got upset with me for being upset with him for feeding the dog too late and then not cleaning up the pee and poo accident on the floor. That night, I slept upstairs in the bedroom while he slept downstairs on the couch. The next morning we didn't speak to one another. We just walked around in silence as I got ready for work. To my surprise but not really, I guess, he was gone when I got home from work.

He left the key I had given him on the bed.

Somehow we managed to get past another bump just in time for Thanksgiving dinner at my sister's house in North Carolina. Now, you must know that my friends and family didn't care much for The Embellisher, but tolerated him for my sake. On this particular occasion, he was just downright strange. We were gathered around the table about to bless the food, and as we all closed in to hold hands, he put his behind his back. His excuse was that he was sick, which was true, but that was one of the rudest things I ever witnessed. My sister and I had had a conversation back in October during my birthday party, as we observed his behavior. Being a licensed clinician, her "diagnosis" was Asperger's, but without proper evaluation – it was just an educated guess.

Once again, my attitude was resigned to accepting him flaws and all. We were only there for a couple days since my sister's boyfriend had flown in from Texas to see her. I wanted to give them some alone time. Besides, The Embellisher had put in for leave to come up to Virginia that following week. Things were okay with us, but it doesn't take a genius (and shouldn't have then, either) to know that this relationship wouldn't last forever.

I was not then aware that the next week up in Virginia would be our last time together. With Christmas only a few weeks away, I still hadn't bought or decided on any gifts for him. That was so not me. My creative juices always run wild and hot around the holidays. This had me worried because I should have been more on the ball. Something was going on in my head, and I needed to figure it out.

We had already planned on taking leave for the last week in December and the first week in January to spend the holidays in Virginia. When he left that last time, I tried to figure out what was happening. I knew really, but just didn't want to deal with it. I loved him, so I didn't want to hurt him, and at the same time I was comfortable with him and didn't want to start all over again. So instead of talking through it with him, I chose to shut myself off for a couple days. When he called, I did not answer, and that wasn't fair to him. Before we hung up the phone that Friday night, he could tell that something was wrong because he told me that he loved me, which is something that I would usually say first.

The very next night, he emailed me, calling things off. Initially, I was relieved that I didn't have to do it, but it still hurt all the same. Then he sent another email with more details about how he felt about me and the whole relationship. He spoke more in that email than in our whole time of dating. Why would he wait until now to start opening up to me? I wrote back stating that I agreed with his decision to go our separate ways and to take care.

This prompted yet another email saying that he wanted to talk and would call me the next day at work. This phone call would be an opportunity for us to mend fences or say our goodbyes for good. It started off with him apologizing for being so hasty in breaking off the relationship because that was not what he really wanted. This was my chance to hold on if that was what I really wanted, but I couldn't. The words were just not there. How could I love this man so dearly and not know what to say? Later that night, we had one more phone call, and it was over.

Not so fast. This is me we're talking about after all, so now we have to talk about my post-breakup issues, right?

After a few days of cell-phone silence and an empty bed, I went into panic mode. My own flaws and

172

faults were staring me directly in the face. Bored and nosy, I decided to get back on the site where he and I met. There he was in his entire splendor, with the exact same ad (still minus the truth), back on the market. This sent me into a tizzy.

I immediately picked up the phone to call him, but he didn't answer. A couple days later he called me, and I foolishly asked him if he still loved me. He managed to elude the question for a while, and then he finally gave me a simple "No." He said that he was fine with the way things were and wanted to focus on himself.

This did not bode well with me, but I wished him well and hung up the phone. I shed my first tear since the breakup. It was time to let go and walk away. Wrong. I managed to stay in contact a little over the next couple weeks. New Year's Eve was looming, and not only did I dread the ball drop, but it also hashed up feelings from the previous New Year's Eve spent alone and waiting on him.

Against my better judgment, I told The Embellisher that this would be a good time to start fresh and new. I didn't know that this is exactly what he was doing, but with someone else! Even still, he told me he was on his way to Florida and would contact me upon his return.   Surprisingly, he did call on his drive back to North Carolina. He talked about visiting his eldest son and his parents, about going shopping, and even sent me pictures that he had taken while he was down there.

New Year's Eve came and went, so I decided to make a random trip down to North Carolina the following weekend. I told him that I was visiting and that maybe we could see each other while I was there. At the beginning of that week, I graciously sent him a dozen white roses with a card that said, "Just something to make you smile." At this point, I must interject that yes, I am well aware, *now*, that my behavior was pretty sad. At the time, I wasn't worried about how it looked on the outside.

Accepting responsibility of one's shortcomings is a hard lesson that I'm still trying to master. Of course there was no meeting that weekend, but inevitably a long tearful ride back home. I finally had to face the fact that it was really over. The brat in me couldn't have what she wanted. To top it off, after traveling up and down that highway for ten years, on this particular trip down, I got my first speeding ticket in Petersburg, Virginia. See? This was a clear sign that my butt should never have made that trip!

I was able to talk to my sister during the drive, and she did her best to console me from a distance. I was a mess, but by the time I reached home, things felt better. I was exhausted and ready for bed. "Tomorrow will be a new day, and I will just start over again."

I was just about to doze off. *Ring...* I reached over, and it was The Embellisher calling. I paused a minute, knowing that the right thing to do was just let it go, but the curious cat in me just had to hear what he had to say. In the most pathetic tone, he asked me why I was able to accept the fact that he had 3 children by 3 different women and had been married twice.

Then, the reason for this question... you guessed it. After seeing this new lady for a couple weeks, he still had not dropped the bomb on her about his children – until that weekend. Since she had already taken him to meet her family for Christmas, she was more than a little ticked off at his deception.

Nevertheless, he needed someone to talk to, so I was the one he called. A couple days later, he called again to give me details of his new love. She was thirty-nine years old, pretty, owned her own business and home (no need for him to buy his own if she has one!), didn't have any children (and he was willing to break his rule and have one with her if she wants), and he wanted to take her home to meet his mother. The average woman would have cursed him out and hung up the phone, but "No, not I," said the duck. I allowed myself to sit there on the other end of the phone and take it. Crazy? Yes!

The next call that came in had a different ringtone and was from a different number. It was The Embellisher again. He had changed his phone number because the drama had already begun between him and his new girlfriend. He apologized for calling and telling me about her. He also told me that it made him realize how good things were when we were together. Oh, and I forgot to mention him saying, "I wonder what it would have been like to take a black woman home to meet my parents." That in itself was grounds enough for me never to speak with him again.

Then the calls stopped for a few days. Lo and behold, the next call that came through was his girlfriend. Cursing and calling him every name under the sun, telling me how she doesn't have time for a project like him. "He's a psychopath, deadbeat dad and a pathological liar"; oh, and she informs me that the flowers that I sent him the week before… he gave them to her for a gift – as if he had bought them. By the way, he didn't see a problem with doing so. When I finally got the chance to ask him about it, he simply said "I didn't feel right throwing them away."

Again, I knew trouble was brewing because I had just come home and had an email from The Embellisher showing me his new tattoo that he got to cover up the name of his ex-fiancé. To make matters worse, it was five o'clock in the morning, and he was required to sign in at school in Maryland by one o'clock that afternoon. How was this my problem, you ask? It wasn't, but I couldn't just sit idly by and watch him jeopardize his career. Well... I could have, but I didn't. Face it, he had four mouths to feed, his and his three children, but all he wanted to do was get some sleep and try to change the date he was due in school (yeah, right).

I told him to suck it up and get his junk together. For the next eight hours, I stayed on the phone with him until he pulled onto the post with only fifteen minutes to spare. Too nice, or too stupid for my own good. It's okay. You can say it. I won't be offended.

Later that night The Embellisher made one last call to me, asking me to hit him over the head with a bat because she had called him and he had lied, again, this time about talking with me while he was driving up to school. His reasoning for this was that he thought that

179

there was still a chance for them. This was the beginning of my checking out.

I'd always been the easy-going, "what's she so happy about?" kind of girl, and optimistic about life, until that following weekend. The Bachelor called me up and asked if I wanted to hang out with him and some of his friends at a bike show in DC. I thought it would be a good idea to get me out of the house.

I went, and was actually having a pretty good time. Everyone was very nice, and there were tons of people around, but for the first time in my life, I felt completely alone. I couldn't understand how or why I was feeling the way I did. All I wanted to do was get out of there and cry. Home couldn't come fast enough, and on my drive back, once everyone was dropped off the floodgates opened and tears began to flow. Knowing that something was just not right, I called my therapist, whom I had not seen in almost a year. It was

Sunday, so I knew I would have to wait a while, but something had to be done. Given our rapport and her knowledge of my personality, her office called me the next day with an afternoon appointment to see her.

The instant I walked into her office, I lost all composure. I could see the worry on her face through my tears, and could tell that her heart was hurting for me as if she were looking at her own child. It was hard for me to begin, but ultimately I admitted that for the first time in my life I was truly lost and needed help.

I explained my daily routine of work, home, then bed, and we both knew that there had been a change in my emotional state. We agreed that, like it or not, pharmaceutical therapy was of the utmost importance for me to get back on track. There was no denying what was happening to me: I was suffering from clinical depression. I had seen it, read about it and studied it. Still, I was clueless as to the inner workings of it. This was crap. The idea of "snap out of it" or "just give it a few days" is absurd.

By night's end, I had taken my first dose of medicine. I took the next couple days off work to relax and adjust to the new meds.

Unfortunately, on day two of my hiatus, The Embellisher's girlfriend decided to call me again and yes, I answered. She wanted to let me know that she was headed up to Maryland to visit him at school for the weekend. She hoped they could try to work things, out and she wanted me to give them space to fix their relationship. I reassured her that I would not be contacting him under any circumstances, so she didn't have to worry about my interfering.

I spent the next few weeks dealing with what was going on in my life. I also had to decide whether to take the Vegas trip that I already paid for, or chalk it up as a loss. After much thought and several talks with my sister and close friends, I decided to go for it. I had the flight and the car reserved, so the only thing left to do was book my hotel room.

Now, the hardest part of this trip was not that it was supposed to be with The Embellisher, but the time of year for which it was scheduled. In my vulnerable and fragile state, I would be in Sin City on Valentine's Day, alone. However, instead of curling into a little ball, I pulled up my big girl panties and prepared to board a plane on the ninth of February.

I confirmed arrangements with The Bachelor to take me to the airport on the night before the flight. I did my last minute check of reservations on the computer when… a message popped up from none other than The Embellisher. For whatever reason, he felt the need to tell me that he graduated from his school and would be heading back home. I sarcastically reminded him that it was all thanks to me. He agreed, and the conversation ended.

The sky was a bright blue and the red of the desert was breathtaking. My trip was just beginning, and I was determined to make it one to remember. Although most people go to Vegas for the drinking and gambling, I was more intrigued by the architecture and surrounding sites. It was imperative that my camera was fully charged and ready to go. After getting into my rental car, I headed straight for the hotel, checked in and settled myself on the twenty-first floor with a spectacular view of the mountains and the Vegas strip.

I was exhausted from the trip because, depression or not, I am still a woman, so the two suitcases, carry-on and computer bag I toted from the airport to the car rental place and then through the hotel casino took their toll on me. All I wanted was food and the nice cool feeling of the sheets in my spacious king-sized bed. I had many plans for the days ahead and needed my rest before getting started.

It's true that there is no need to leave your hotel in Vegas; food, shopping, shows… mine even had rides on the roof. I had promised my daughter to document the entire trip photographically, so I faithfully posted several pictures on Facebook each day. I did spend a fair share of time in my room, but also ventured out to a comedy show at the Flamingo and to a concert at the infamous Caesar's Palace, where I got a hug and kiss from the very cute and sexy, blue-eyed Matt Goss. If you are unaware who he is, look him up. I promise you will not be disappointed, and he has a marvelous velvet voice.

Moving on, my next venture was to the Grand Canyon, followed by the Hoover Dam on the way back. I never imagined the absolute beauty of these two wonders. The sounds, the silence, the colors, the majesty of it all will forever be a part of me, from the roads I traveled to get there to the remarkable shots I captured on my camera.

I also checked out another spot right down from the strip called Red Rock Canyon. This site consisted of a 13-mile road that you could drive down, with designated stopping points for viewing and picture taking. To my surprise, after my fourth day there, I had already put over 400 miles on my rental car.

I managed to fit a little gambling in while I was there, but that wasn't high on my list of things to do. Besides visiting the surrounding area, taking pictures and shopping were of utmost importance. I wanted to bring back a very special gift for my sweet girl, and what better way to express my love for her then jewelry wrapped in a cute little blue box from Tiffany's? I knew she would be overjoyed when I gave it to her on my return.

I was so glad I had decided to take the trip after all.

Although I had some extremely memorable moments while I was there, I also experienced times of sorrow and sadness. Passing the hotel where he and I were supposed to have stayed, or the sight of hearts and flowers set up for the pending holiday – these things were difficult. Nights alone crying in my bed were all part of the healing process, so my attitude was to let it out, and tomorrow would be a new day when I would be that much closer to feeling better.

I feel the need to interject here that, with all the chaos and turmoil of my past and present, I had made contact with The Charmer again. To add to the unhealthiness of my situation, he was supplying me with the comfort and tough love needed for the predicament I now found myself in.

It felt good to be home again. There's always that special feeling of being back around the familiar, and sleeping in your own bed. My daughter and I caught up while she opened the goodies I'd brought back for her. Just as I expected, the look on her face when I handed her the little blue bag was priceless.

I was scheduled to work the next day but, since I had got in so late, I decided to stay out just a little longer and rest up from the trip. I was still trying to put things into perspective, and I made a conscious decision to sit down and write an email to The Embellisher. Yeah, yeah, I know… whatever! I detailed my trip out west, what was going on in my life, and how I was feeling. I explained to him how hard it had been to take a trip we had planned together, and that I had done it despite the pain.

His response detailed the turmoil of his new relationship and how he had wondered whether or not I'd taken the trip alone. He offered to compensate me for a portion of the funds that I spent, but of course I declined.

Over the next couple of months, the lines of communication remained open between the two of us. The sole purpose of this was for him to have an ear to bend when things were crazy in North Carolina. First, he sent a strange message one night via instant chat about his girlfriend choking him and hitting him as they were driving to dinner. That's madness, right? He claimed to have pulled over, taken pictures of his neck and called the police and his First Sergeant. The next day at work he called me and said that he couldn't believe he was putting up with her behavior. It was over. I told him that he wasn't going anywhere and that he would no doubt forgive her – which he did.

Things were starting to mellow out for me. I was getting out and about again. The smile on my face returned, and I was back on the dating scene. It had been about two weeks since I'd heard from The Embellisher, which was good for my mind and my forward progression. Then came that day in April when I came out of my therapist appointment to find five missed calls, three text messages and one voice mail from… you guessed it, The Embellisher.

Seriously, I couldn't do anything but laugh, at first. Then, just as I'd done every time before, I called to see what the problem was. In a nutshell, they had got into a fight, and she was trying to hit him, so he kicked her in the butt and told her to leave. Now, the remarkable part of this story was him in his truck, up the road in a parking lot, afraid to go home for fear of her calling the cops on him for kicking her.

Really dude? You are right where and with whom you wanted to be. There was nothing I could say to him that was going to change his situation, so contacting me was a waste of his time and mine. It's funny to think that I was the only one in therapy.

The next day, I realized it was time to sever the ties. I drafted a message to The Embellisher expressing my regret that he was in such an unhealthy relationship but that I no longer wanted to be a part of it. I wished him well and told him to lose my phone number. Pushing the send button on that email was profound. It had taken me way too long, but now it was done I could focus on my future and not my past. In that moment, I came to realize why this particular relationship hit me so hard upon its ending.

I have always known that I give more then I receive with my partners, but my main problem was the fear of not being needed. It wasn't that I loved him so much that I couldn't live without him; on the contrary, it was that I was going to have to start all over again and find someone who needed me. This mode of thinking is what I started to work on, because I no longer wanted to be with a man who needed me. I just wanted a man that appreciated, deserved and wanted me back.

CHAPTER 4
Finding My Place in This World

The April showers brought beautiful May flowers into my life. With prayer, positive thinking, good friends and family, my world has gotten back in alignment. Although I'm impaired when it comes to choosing a man, my family and friendship base is immeasurable. My sisters and I are best friends. No matter what the dilemma, all we have to do is reach out, and a loving heart and a helpful hand will be there.

Proof of this unconditional love was the decision to have a sisters' weekend at the conclusion of my meltdown. It was better than what a doctor could have ordered. We got dressed up, went dancing and, all at the same time yet in separate rooms, had permanent artwork etched into our skin. This may seem slightly contrived, but this would be my last one. It was my older sister's first time. And my younger sister, who practically lives in the parlor, improved on one of her eleven existing pictures. This family affair was priceless, and it's reassuring to know that my faults, mistakes and bad choices are not judged by those close to me. My friendships span the United States and are decades strong.

After four months of assistance from a little yellow pill, I informed my therapist that I was done. Most people rely on this aid for a year or more, but I was ready to deal with life head on once again. This decision was prompted by the death of my dearest friend's son. In May 2011, he was laid to rest at the age of fourteen. As I stood there, seeing him lie lifeless in the casket, there were no tears. I wanted to mourn his life, I needed to grieve his death, but I couldn't because of the medication. That day, I stopped taking that little yellow pill. Being who I am, I would rather feel pain and discomfort than nothing at all.

It's amazing how the hard times in life make us so much stronger. I have a new outlook, new rules and yes, the rules of love in my life have changed. I'm not afraid of putting my heart out there at all, but if I sense that the man is not worthy, I erase. Most live by the three-strike rule, but I now allow just two strikes. Considering I don't even like baseball, I have altered the play book.

On the first strike, shame on you, after the second strike, shame on me – he's out, plain and simple. The funny thing with this is the surprised tone when, after a week or so of no contact, they reach out and I ask, "Who is this?" You see, I have already deleted the contact. I'm done. I have no desire to waste my time or anyone else's.

I feel it's important to give a little insight into my lifelong dating preference. I have only ever dated interracially. My ex-husband was Mexican, and the men who followed were all white. To me this has never been a big deal, but the looks still exist, even today. I get questions like, "Why only white men?" And I get statements like, "You just haven't found the right black man to show you how you deserve to be treated."

I'll tell you a secret, that last statement was spoken to me by a black man who felt I should know my worth, as a black woman. And, given the chance, he could be just the man to prove his words. Did I mention that this helpful soul was married, with children?

I always thought that all the abuse and turmoil at the hands of a black man that I witnessed during my upbringing was the reason I have never chosen one for my life partner. Now, at the age of forty, I am well aware that good men, as well as bad men, come in all shades and colors. But at the end of the day, it just comes down to who you are and aren't attracted to.

The dating scene is the same as when I left it back in 2009. Those of you who have been in and out of said trenches will know it is truly exhausting. Dinner, movies, small talk, random walks or whatever else has been planned – it's all tiring. I've found that my tolerance for BS has diminished

Also, in a world of such vast resources and opportunity, I find it utterly amazing that the male population has a difficult time reading and comprehending the written language. No matter how specific a woman might be about what she wants, some men view themselves as exempt from those wants and desires. On many occasions I've asked the simple question, "Did you read what I wrote?" and have received various responses rather than a straightforward Yes or No.

Seriously, get off my phone or my computer, whichever medium I happen to be using at the time.

One might think this shortcoming is reserved to a specific type of man, but it's not. Laborer, soldier, lawyer, business owner, doctor – I have spoken cordially with, and dated, all of them.

Since I had some free time on my hands, along with sorting out the baggage of my past, I decided to test out a few theories about the whole online dating thing. Wow, the World Wide Web is fascinating, to say the least. I explored three different sites, one that charged a fee and two that were free. Oddly enough, I found several of the same people in all three places, with completely contradictory requests. These discoveries prompted me to question and address the reasoning for this method.

Most did not get offended when I brought this to their attention, but I did recommend that they adjust their intentions so as to not mislead a fellow searcher such as myself. The other interesting element of online dating is the people who suggest not telling those who ask how you met. Really! So, from the very beginning, we should make up a lie? What a great foundation for the start of a healthy, fulfilling new relationship!

Because of the accessibility and relative convenience of online dating, not to mention that it provides an avenue for women to make the untraditional "first move", people can hide and omit what they like for the sake of attracting more hits. This is very similar to real life, of course, except that we forfeit the opportunity to witness body language and the visual cues of deceit.

I'm still learning that life is ever-changing. Just when you think you have it figured out, a new challenge arises. The key is to take one day at a time, and don't try to anticipate what might come next.

Plans are a good thing as long as the parameters surrounding them aren't so rigid that catastrophe strikes when they change.

In the past, I have always just rolled with the punches, but even the most seasoned fighter wears and tatters after a while. I think that is what happened to me. It was time for me to return to my corner. I was in dire need of rest, water and a stool.

Although this book started as a therapeutic project, it quickly took on a life of its own. With each word, sentence, paragraph and page that spilled from me, I discovered more of who I am and what I am all about. Besides, I've always heard that everyone has at least one book in them. It's just about having the ability and taking the time to put it down on paper.

We all have room for improvement, and can take lessons from our past. I love who I am, and though I have made plenty of mistakes and bad choices, I'm still here. I haven't given up. I still walk with my head held high, and I feel more blessed than ever.

Oddly enough, someone recently asked me if there was anything about the men I dated that I missed. After a little thought, I couldn't think of anything profound enough to make me want to change my life's natural progression. It's strange how such a simple question can provide such clarity.

As far as I have come in this whole process, there are still things that I need to address, such as, how do I break from the patterns that I have followed for so many years? What steps do I take in order to live for my future and let the past be just that, the past?

Although this story details some of the actions of people who have been a part of my life, that is not the main topic for me. My focus throughout this writing was to document how I ignored obvious unhealthy patterns, provide visual evidence of what my mistakes have been, and do the work necessary to change the destructive habits.

It's true that everything happens for a reason, and certain people are brought in and out of our lives on purpose. We are all connected in one way or another. Through all of life's experiences, we are shaped and molded into these diverse and interesting individuals. And throughout this process, we consciously and unconsciously keep little parts of those who have touched us in some way.

In the same manner, we leave pieces of ourselves behind as those people disappear from our lives. I've always wondered how someone can give their heart and soul to another without completely losing sight of their own best interests. In giving up so much, how do they maintain the health of their relationships and also their emotional wellness?"

I have no doubt that this is possible, but for me, I think I put too much focus on the happiness and well-being of the other person. It's a known fact that we are not responsible for, nor can we control this, within another. But what I know and how I act are two entirely different things. Yes, I am fully aware that I have displayed selfish tendencies when establishing some of my relationships. For that I am ashamed, and know that I will have to answer for those choices that I've made.

My ultimate goal is to stop worrying so much about what others want and concentrate on what I want and what is going to be best for me. A good example of this is a conversation that I had with my sister about writing this book. As I began to tell her about some of its content, I expressed my concerns about possible backlash from family. She quickly told me not to worry about any of that. Her position was that this was for me and no one else, so if someone has something to say about it, too bad. She also pointed out that I was still being "too nice" with my story, but I feel strongly that its purpose was not to blame or shame anyone for the things that transpired in the past.

Though my biggest fear in writing this story was the pain it might cause my parents once they had a chance to read it, I still forged on. Would it make them sad? Would they feel they had failed us kids in some way? Then one day I was out walking around and realized: despite the abuse, the constant relocation and the all-around dysfunction, we all survived – not unscathed, but relevant.

So many times the outcome is tragic. But in our case, there were no high school dropouts; no teenage pregnancies; no drug abuse. We have all earned degrees in the health field: a doctor of psychology, a nurse, and me with a BA in psychology, having also served my country in the United States Army.

We turned our negatives into positives. It may sound strange, but our desire to help those around us came from them. The developmental years of our lives, though unconventional, formulated our course. I want them to be thankful for who we are and how far we have risen. It is important for them to know that our climb is not over, not even close.

It would be so simple to look at the things that have transpired in my life with despair, but that would be too easy. The reflections, the lessons that I've received from this ordeal are what I did to myself – the choices and decisions that I made. I'm the one who made the conscious decision to involve myself in adulterous relationships. I should have known better after seeing the repercussions of said actions though my parents' participating in the same type of behavior.

Without experience, there cannot be testimony, and I am here to tell you that Karma is real. The focus cannot rest on others, its place is with me and how I intend to take complete responsibility for the imprint I leave in this life. Everything that has happened in My First Forty Years was all part of a plan. We all have one, and though we may not know what it means or how it will end, everything is a part of that plan.

I once heard that if we were to ask God to explain this plan to us, we would not even begin to understand His logic and wisdom behind it. With all the people, places and things involved, it would be like trying to put together a five thousand piece jigsaw puzzle blindfolded, with one hand tied behind your back, in the desert with no water.

At the end of the day, I must assume full responsibility. This is my life, my story, my journey. Good and bad, it all belongs to me. Will I ever make another wrong decision? Of course I will. Why? It's because there is no such thing as "perfect" in this world. We are all imperfect people with personal opinions, habits and flaws. This is what makes our lives so full, unique and great. How wonderful it is to have such a vast array of ideas and characters to watch, learn from, read about and marvel at!

This may sound a little harsh, but just when you think you have it bad; there is always someone even worse off than you. It's sad but true. This simple fact reminds me of a song that I heard while in the midst of my depression: "Smile", by Kirk Franklin. I was on my way to work one morning when this song came on the radio. Music has always had a very special meaning and place in my heart, but on this particular day, it was amplified. The words and tone of this song instantly changed the expression on my face. I did what the song told me to do. I smiled.

The reminder that nobody can take my joy was ever-present, and I smiled, clapped and sang that song all the way to the commuter lot. And you know what? For a week straight, every morning when I got in my truck to head to the lot for work, that song played on my radio. This to me was another demonstration that "God may not always give us what we want, but He is faithful in giving us what we need." At that particular time in my life, I needed that song more than anything.

To be in a loving and healthy relationship is still something I want and desire, but I now view being single as a positive moment. Don't get me wrong, I scan the prospects, along with all the other single ladies. I have even met a couple who I would keep for my very own given the chance, but I'm patient and willing to be still until the right one, not the perfect one but the right one, comes along.

As I wait for what is meant to be, time is not lost as I once believed; it is gained. This is an opportunity for me to stop and think about what I really want, not just in my personal life, but all of it. I've been fortunate in my time to have held a lot of positions that have afforded me the opportunity to learn many different skill sets. Gaining a little more clarity during this phase of my life, I am honing in on a few of them for future advancement.

Today, I am happy to report that a smile is a permanent fixture on my face, once again. Yes, the silly care-free woman that I was before all of this began has returned. No meds, no hatred or bitterness exists, nor am I embarrassed about what I went through or the decision I made to seek help. Surprisingly, I haven't had a problem talking about what I went through this year either.

Part of this is without question due to my being a woman and having the gift of gab, but the main reason is, it is life. This is my life, and if someone is going to get to know me, they need to know where I've been and where I'm going. It wasn't weakness that got me here; it was strength, faith and love.

My future partner must know that I am not one to fall and stay down. Blood, sweat and tears, my spirit is strong, and no matter what life throws at me, it will not keep me down forever. I have been on dates where I brought up the fact that I was writing a memoir, and they usually said, "Wow, Really? When is your book going to be done, and can I read it?"

So when I finish (and if you're reading this, I guess I did), there are quite a few copies already spoken for.

Another interesting find in all of this is that I can now say out loud what I don't want. The long laundry list that I see women make for that special someone – I had never made one. Even today, it is not written, but I know what goes on it. I cannot be with a man who wants children other than the ones he may already have, and mine. He must display a genuine love for his role as their father. I cannot be with a man who is looking to get out, in the process of getting out, or almost out of a legally binding contract. I am only available to give myself to someone who is just as single as I am.

This journey of life that I am on never stops surprising me. I wake up every morning and thank God that He has given me another day. This project opened my eyes to so many things that at times get a bit overwhelming. Never in a million years would I have imagined that I, the girl who hated school, the one who would wait until the night before it was due to complete a ten-page paper for class, would write an entire book of my very own. True, it covers a subject of which I have first-hand knowledge, but I finished it. That's what makes this different from so many of the projects that I have started and later set aside.

This venture has also taught me that I need to be more thankful. It's crucial that I work on being a better person so the decisions I make cause little or no damage to the ones I love and who love me. I also see that I already have the most important things in life: faith, my daughter, family and my health.

My forty-first birthday is quickly approaching and I am looking forward to growing another year younger. Since I still get carded when I order a drink, I have a strong defense for using that previous statement! Also, my baby girl is about to celebrate her sweet sixteen. We are talking college and our plan for relocation out of the Northern Virginia area in a few years.

Its' funny how time just flies when you're living life. I still remember the moment that little angel was placed in my arms for the first time. I worried and wondered if I would be a good mother, and tried to imagine what she would be when she grew up. There was always the vision of her father and I attending high school and college graduations, the two of us helping to plan and arrange the day that she would walk down the aisle to begin a life of her own. Never did the idea of divorce or death enter my mind. For much of the fourteen years since the divorce and the nine years since his death, I had been trying to erase the stigma of "single black mother"; what I couldn't see was that it was who I am, not all that I am, but an important part.

My ex-husband would always reassure me that I would do an excellent job at raising our daughter. There was no doubt in his mind about it. Sometimes I wonder if sharing the love that I had with him has somehow tainted the waters for those who have come after him. He once told me that no matter where I go or who I am with, in life or in death, I would always be his wife and he would always be my husband.

Some Friendships Are for Always

We've shared the kind of friendship

That's grown deeper through the years,

We've seen the ups; we've known the downs,

We've shared the smiles and tears,

And through it all, I've learned one thing –

That there could never be

A dearer friend in all the world

Than the one you are to me.

Emily Matthews

The significance behind this poem is that it is written on a wallet-sized card that my ex-husband gave to me before he died. I have kept it in my wallet for the past nine years, except for a time when I realized that my daughter had decided to take possession of it for a while. I made this discovery one day when I was going through her purse for something that she needed. As soon as I spotted the card, I couldn't help but smile. You see, she knows its meaning as well, so to share it with her increased its value for the both of us.

What I have come to realize is that I am a strong, intelligent, loving, stubborn, determined woman who has made some bad decisions in my life, yet I have made plenty of good ones, too. I wisely chose to leave an unhealthy marriage even though it meant that I would become a statistic. I am a devoted and wonderful mother who lost the father of her child, which meant it was solely up to me to nourish, guide and love her enough for two people. This task at hand has been my most challenging job thus far. But I am here to tell you, being her mother, caregiver, mentor and friend has been absolutely amazing. The young lady I call daughter continues to strive and flourish, despite all her mother's oopsies. She is my purpose. She has proudly stood by my side every step of the way, held my hand and told me, "We are not alone – because we have the help of God to get us through."

Epilogue

I was so *excited* and *terrified,* to be embarking upon this new adventure. It was time for me to step out of my comfort zone and do something a little different. Sure, I had worn the uniform but I had never traveled beyond the gates of Fort Bragg for the call of duty. This was going to be an opportunity to see just how strong I truly am. Being away from Boogie, is going to be very difficult. I just have to keep telling myself, "Everything is going to be okay".

I'm startled awake from the *'DING'* of the cabins fasten seat belt indicator. I don't even remember falling asleep. I guess it could be a result of the two little pills that my doctor gave me specifically for this trip. Everyone is now milling about the plane gathering up all their belongings and issued gear. As I stand to make my way to the front exit door… this unbelievable heat, literally, smacks me in my face. "What in the Hell have I gotten myself into"?

It was 6:30 in the evening, but the temperature outside felt like I was walking on the sun. Having completed an extensive physical examination, a massive amount of paperwork, seven days of training in the Georgia heat and eighteen hours in the friendly skies…I had finally arrived at my transitional place, Kuwait. Lugging my belongings down the sandy pathway, all I could do was pray that I made it to a building or tent that had an ample supply of water and air conditioning. An irrational thought crossed my mind, "Can you keel over from heat exhaustion after only five minutes of walking under the Middle Eastern sun?... Nah" but I quickly made my way inside because I didn't want to find out.

Well… this was only the beginning and I needed to get used to being a little uncomfortable.

Being this was my first time out of the country, everything seemed so surreal. Most people would have opted for Mexico or the Caribbean as their Segway into jet setting but I never seem to follow the easiest paths in life, so why wouldn't I start my new journey by volunteering to support the warfighter for six months in Afghanistan.

26943442R00123